# MANAGING YOUR MONEY

# MANAGING YOUR MONEY

### Anthea Masey

KOGAN PAGE

## Acknowledgements

The author thanks the following for kind permission to reproduce illustrations: Barclays Bank plc, Halifax Building Society, HM-Stationery Office, Lloyds Bank plc, and National Westminster Bank.

## The author

Anthea Masey is a freelance financial journalist who has worked on *Which?*, *Evening News* and the *Daily Mail* (City Desk)

Copyright © Anthea Masey 1988

All rights reserved. No reproduction, copy or transmission of this publication may be made without written permission.

No paragraph of this publication may be reproduced, copied or transmitted save with written permission or in accordance with the provisions of the Copyright Act 1956 (as amended), or under the terms of any licence permitting limited copying issued by the Copyright Licensing Agency, 7 Ridgmount Street, London WC1E 7AE.

Any person who does any unauthorised act in relation to this publication may be liable to criminal prosecution and civil claims for damages.

First published in Great Britain in 1988 by
Kogan Page Limited, 120 Pentonville Road,
London N1 9JN

**British Library Cataloguing in Publication Data**

Masey, Anthea
  Managing your money: the Daily Mail guide.
  1. Great Britain. Personal finance
  I. Title
  332.024'00941

  ISBN 1-85091-716-7

Typeset by DP Photosetting, Aylesbury, Bucks
Printed and bound in Great Britain by
Biddles Limited, Guildford

# CONTENTS

| | | |
|---|---|---|
| **1** | **Your Pay** | **9** |
| | Your payslip | 9 |
| | The deductions | 12 |
| | Cumulative tax records | 14 |
| | | |
| **2** | **The Inland Revenue** | **17** |
| | Pay As You Earn | 17 |
| | Personal allowances | 18 |
| | Checking your Notice of Coding | 20 |
| | Checking your tax bill | 22 |
| | How much tax do I pay? | 24 |
| | Working for yourself | 25 |
| | The tax return | 28 |
| | How to appeal | 31 |
| | Tax and marriage | 31 |
| | | |
| **3** | **Where to Keep Your Cash** | **34** |
| | Bank current accounts | 34 |
| | Credit cards | 43 |
| | The cost of running a bank current account | 44 |

|   |   |   |
|---|---|---|
|   | What else can you do at the bank? | 46 |
|   | The electronic age | 48 |
|   | Financial fraud | 48 |
| 4 | **Budgeting** | **50** |
|   | Monitor your spending | 50 |
|   | Control your credit cards | 51 |
|   | Save for bills | 51 |
|   | Spreading costs | 52 |
|   | Budget planner | 53 |
| 5 | **Saving** | **56** |
|   | Regular savings plans | 61 |
|   | Lump sum investment | 67 |
|   | Becoming an investor | 71 |
|   | Investment information | 76 |
|   | How to complain | 77 |
| 6 | **Borrowing Money** | **82** |
|   | Comparing rates of interest | 82 |
|   | Where to borrow? | 84 |
|   | The law on credit | 91 |
| 7 | **Insurance** | **93** |
|   | How much insurance do you need? | 94 |
|   | Family income plans | 97 |
|   | How much lump sum insurance? | 99 |
|   | What else is on offer? | 101 |
|   | Sickness insurance | 103 |
|   | Buildings and contents insurance | 107 |
| 8 | **Going Abroad** | **115** |
|   | Your holiday checklist | 115 |

|   |   |   |
|---|---|---|
|   | Holiday insurance | 118 |
|   | Car breakdown and recovery insurance | 119 |
|   | Holiday money | 119 |

## 9  Buying a Home — 124
- How much can you borrow? — 126
- How much does it cost to move? — 126
- Where to go for a mortgage — 129
- Finding the right mortgage — 131
- Repayment mortgages — 131
- Endowment mortgages — 133
- Pension mortgages — 133
- The buying process — 141
- Making a will — 143

## 10  Retirement — 148
- State pension — 148
- Company pension schemes — 149
- Public sector schemes — 153
- The State Earnings-Related Pension Scheme — 153
- State graduated scheme — 155
- Personal pensions — 155
- Additional voluntary contributions — 157

## Appendices — 161
1. Useful Addresses — 163
2. Useful Leaflets — 167

## Personal Finance Titles from Kogan Page — 169

## Index of Advertisers — 171

# Managed Financial Services Ltd

INVESTMENT, INSURANCE & MORTGAGE CONSULTANTS

- MORTGAGES ● COMMERCIAL FINANCE
- RE-MORTGAGES ● PERSONAL
- HOUSEHOLD INSURANCE ● PENSIONS
- SELF EMPLOYED HEALTH
- SICKNESS BENEFITS ● INCOME PLANS FOR THE ELDERLY HOMEOWNER
- INVESTMENTS ● UNIT TRUSTS ETC.

*FOR ANY TYPE OF FINANCIAL ADVICE*

**RING: MR ROBERT CHAMBERLAIN**

(0203) 630162

OR WRITE TO:—

8 IRONMONGER ROW, COVENTRY CV1 1FD

---

## KOGAN PAGE

# EASING INTO RETIREMENT

### Keith Hughes

Published in association with  Legal and General

Retirement brings a time of adventure and opportunity, but adjusting successfully to retirement can be difficult without adequate planning and preparation. **Easing into Retirement** is full of factual information and useful advice on how to go about planning your retirement.

£4.95 *( + £1.00 p&p) Paperback*  ISBN 1 85091 302 1
88 pages  216x138mm

# 1
# YOUR PAY

Pay day isn't what it was. The generation which grew up with bank accounts has nothing to replace the excitement of the bulging pay packet with its pound notes and handful of small change stuffed into its small brown envelope.

You are now regarded as something of a freak if you say you want your money in cash and once a week. The weekly pay packet is fast become a folk memory. And if you weren't being paid in cash on 1 January 1987, your employer can now insist on paying you by bank giro credit or by cheque.

The banks say that six out of ten employees are now either paid by cheque or have their money paid straight into a bank account.

Many of them never knew the simple joy of that bulging wad of notes. Celebrating pay day with a payslip somehow isn't the same.

## Your payslip

Do you take one look at your pay before the tax and National Insurance people take their bites and then despair at how little is left after they have had their fill? Don't worry – you are doing just what everyone else does.

Linger over your payslip a bit longer and you might get to love it. It's a good read and contains a wealth of interesting detail.

Save them, they are your record of how much you have paid in tax, National Insurance, pension and union dues. You may not need them now, but you never know when you might get involved in a dispute with the Inland Revenue or the Department of Health and Social Security.

## MANAGING YOUR MONEY

| Date | P'd No. | Name | Tax Code | Dept. | Payroll No. |
|---|---|---|---|---|---|
| 30.5.87 | | VERONICA ORDINARY | 233 L | | |
| Basic Pay | Special Adj. | Special Adj. | Special Adj. | Special Adj. | GROSS PAY |
| 416.66 | | | | | 416.66 |
| Tax | Nat. Ins. | Co. Pension | Other Deds. | | TOTAL DEDS |
| 59.94 | 29.05 | | | | 88.99 |
| Gross to Date | Tax to Date | Nat. Ins. to Date | Co. Pen. to Date | | NET PAY |
| 833.32 | 119.61 | 58.10 | | | 327.67 |

Special Adjustment Codes

1 Overtime
2 Holiday Pay
3 Bonus/Commission
4 Taxable Adj.
5 Non-Taxable Adj.

Figure 1.1 A payslip

Also, it is not unknown for employers to make mistakes, and those mistakes may be costing you money. So don't throw your payslip in the bin, let it reveal its secrets instead.

HOW TO READ YOUR PAYSLIP

Look at the payslip on page 10. It may not be identical to the one you get, but the various headings will be more or less the same.

Most companies pay their employees every month or every week. Monthly pay normally coincides with the calendar month, and weekly pay normally runs from Monday to Sunday.

When you get your payslip, start at the figure for basic pay. If you are paid once a month, you can check it by dividing your annual wages or salary by 12. If you are paid weekly, your annual pay will be divided by 52, even though there are sometimes 53 pay days in the tax year.

If your job pays overtime, and you worked some in the period covered by the payslip, there should be an amount entered in the space for overtime.

You may be entitled to a bonus. Some companies pay a regular bonus at Christmas and ahead of the summer holidays. And if part of your pay is linked to how much you do and how fast you do it, some of your pay is classed as a bonus.

If you are a member of your company's sales team, some or all of your pay may be linked to how much you sell. This is entered under the heading for commission, and the amount fluctuates depending on your performance.

If you are lucky enough to work for a company which carries on paying you for several months after you fall ill, you will continue to get a normal payslip. This looks no different from the one you get while you are working, except you aren't entitled to any overtime, bonuses or commission.

On the other hand, if your pay stops or is reduced as soon as you fall ill, you should be able to find out how much you will get from your *Contract of Employment*. The least you can expect is the amount due to you under the *Statutory Sick Pay* scheme.

Statutory Sick Pay lasts for the first 28 weeks of any illness which keeps you away from work. The money comes via your employer who claims it back from the Department of Health and Social Security.

Most employers who carry on paying during long periods of ill health deduct Statutory Sick Pay from basic pay. Otherwise you could be better off staying at home.

You only get Statutory Sick Pay if your pay, worked out on a weekly basis, is above the level at which you start paying National Insurance contributions. If you are entitled to Statutory Sick Pay it is paid at three different levels, depending on how much you earn each week.

Statutory Sick Pay and money from your employer's sick pay scheme is taxable, and is added to your total gross pay.

## The deductions

Now comes the painful part. Your employer has the unpleasant task of acting as a collector for the Inland Revenue and the Department of Health and Social Security. There may be deductions for pension contributions and union dues as well.

Somewhere on your payslip there will be a figure for your tax code. Your employer uses this to work out how much tax you should be paying. If it's wrong you won't be paying the right amount of tax. And as these things work, it is usually too much. Chapter 2, *The Inland Revenue*, tells you how to make sure your tax code is correct.

There is an entry showing how much tax you paid in the month or week covered by the payslip.

The next big deduction is for National Insurance contributions. Your National Insurance contribution record determines whether or not you have the right to a whole range of state benefits, ranging from unemployment benefit and maternity benefit to the state basic pension and invalidity pension.

The National Insurance contributions you pay depend on your circumstances (see Table 1.1). If you are paying into a company pension scheme or personal pension plan which is approved by the Inland Revenue, you pay less than you do if you remain in the government's Statutory Earnings-Related Pension Scheme (SERPS). If you are a married woman or a widow you may be entitled to pay lower contributions.

But you don't have to pay anything if your earnings are low or you are working past retirement age (60 for women, 65 for men), or if you are less than 16 years old.

Your payslip is your record of what happened in the previous month or week. It also gives you a cumulative picture since the beginning of the tax year which starts on 6 April each year. It shows your gross pay from the beginning of the tax year to the end of the month or week covered by the payslip. You also get the cumulative figures for tax and National Insurance contributions.

If your company runs a company pension scheme, any deduction is shown on your payslip. No two pension schemes are the same, and

**Table 1.1** National Insurance contributions from 6 April 1988

CLASS 1 CONTRIBUTIONS (EMPLOYEES)

*Contributing to the State Earnings Related Pension Scheme (SERPS)*

| Earnings | |
|---|---|
| Below £2,132.00 | Nothing |
| Between £2,132.00 and £3,639.99 a year | 5 per cent |
| Between £3,640.00 and £5,459.99 a year | 7 per cent |
| Between £5,460.00 and £15,859.99 a year | 9 per cent |
| Over £15,860.00 a year | £1,427.40 which is 9 per cent of £15,860.00 |

*Contributing to an Inland Revenue approved company pension scheme*

| Earnings | |
|---|---|
| Below £2,132.00 | Nothing |
| Between £2,132.00 and £3,639.99 a year | 3 per cent[1] |
| Between £3,640.00 and £5,459.99 a year | 5 per cent[1] |
| Between £5,460.00 and £15,859.99 a year | 7 per cent[1] |
| Over £15,860.00 a year | £1,152.84 which is 7 per cent of £15,860.00 plus an extra 2 per cent on the first £2,132. |

[1] There is an extra 2 per cent to pay on the first £2,132.00

CLASS 2 CONTRIBUTIONS (SELF-EMPLOYED)
£4.05 a week

CLASS 3 CONTRIBUTIONS (VOLUNTARY)
£3.95 a week

CLASS 4 CONTRIBUTIONS (SELF-EMPLOYED)
6.3 per cent of profits of gains between £4,750 and £15,860 a year.

some schemes don't ask for any contributions from employees. If you do have to pay into yours, the size of your contribution is normally a percentage of your gross pay, which is by and large the same for all employees. Depending on the scope of the scheme it could be anything between 4 and 6 per cent.

If you are paying in extra under the Additional Voluntary Contributions system your pension contributions can be boosted up to a maximum of 15 per cent of your earnings. This is explained more fully in Chapter 10, *Retirement*.

Payments into an approved company pension scheme are tax free, but National Insurance contributions are paid out of taxed income.

ESTABLISHED 1972 · MEMBERS OF FIMBRA

# AYLESBURY ASSOCIATES

01-464 5416 (5 lines)

*FULL DEALING and ADVISORY SERVICE*

**Stocks and Shares — Unit Trust — Income Bonds
Offshore Accounts — Portfolio Management**

Home Reversion — Income Plans
**PERSONALISED ADVICE ONLY**

FOR INFORMATION WITHOUT OBLIGATION SEND TO:

---

DMG.88

**AYLESBURY ASSOCIATES
FREEPOST
71A HIGH STREET
BROMLEY
KENT BR1 1BR**

NAME ..................................................

ADDRESS ............................................

..............................................................

..............................................................

TELEPHONE NO. ................................

## Cumulative tax records

Soon after the tax year ends, your employer sends you a form known as the P60. This shows your gross pay and the amount of tax your employer handed over to the Inland Revenue on your behalf. You will notice that the figure for gross pay may not tally with the cumulative figure on the last payslip of the tax year. This is because your employer deducts any pension payments, which are tax free, from your gross pay to arrive at a figure on your P60. If you do the same, the figures should tie up.

When you leave a job, your employer gives you a form P45. It gives your new boss all the information needed to carry on taxing you at the correct rate.

So don't just curse the Inland Revenue each time you open your payslip. If you do you are forgetting the sizable sums you hand over in National Insurance and pension contributions. If you are a basic-rate taxpayer, reckon to lose around 25 per cent of your salary once everyone has got their fingers sticky in your honey pot.

YOUR PAY

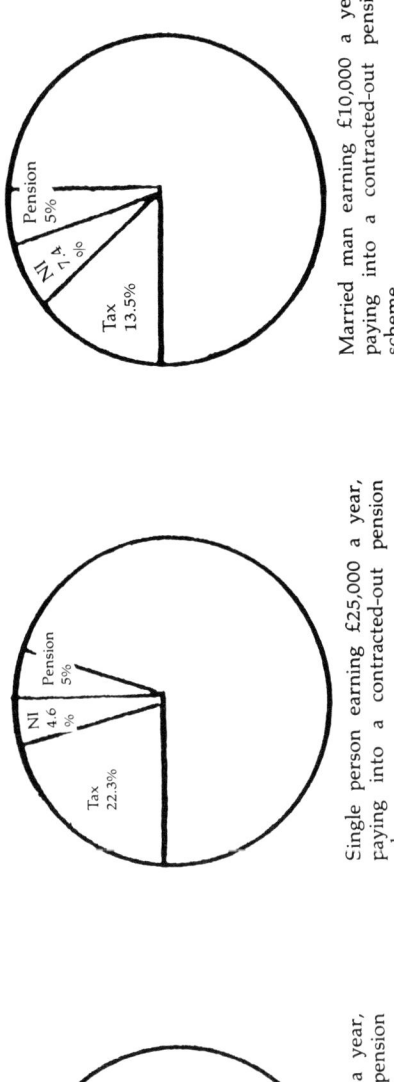

Figure 1.2 Deductions from pay in 1988–89 tax year

## MANAGING YOUR MONEY

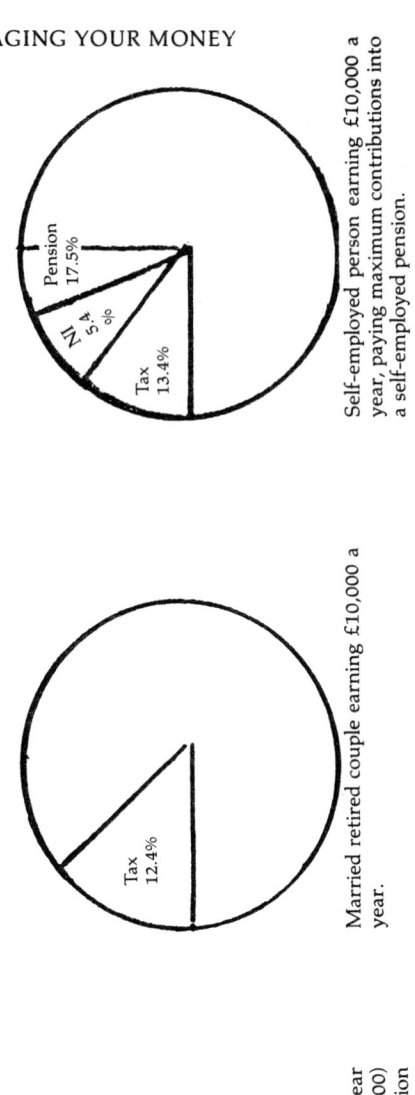

Self-employed person earning £10,000 a year, paying maximum contributions into a self-employed pension.

Married retired couple earning £10,000 a year.

Married couple earning £15,000 a year (husband earning £10,000, wife £5,000) both paying into contracted-out pension schemes.

**Figure 1.2** *Deductions from pay in 1988–89 tax year* (continued).

# 2
# THE INLAND REVENUE

The most important thing to remember about the Inland Revenue is their inefficiency. Letters take months to be answered, files are frequently lost, and tax assessments are usually late.

It's also their most endearing characteristic, because buried under those piles of paper there is a tax inspector struggling to keep track of your finances and several hundred other people's as well.

It follows that anyone armed with a little bit of knowledge and who knows their way round the system stands a good chance of staying ahead of their tax inspector and getting the best possible deal out of the tax system.

Taxes comes in all shapes and sizes. Some tax our income, others tax our spending, and there can be tax to pay when we sell something or give our money away.

Most people cut their tax teeth on income tax. This is the tax you pay on the money you earn, or the income you get from your savings and investments. Everyone from the smallest child to the oldest old-age pensioner can, in theory, get a bill for income tax.

## Pay As You Earn

If you have a job where you work for someone else your pay cheque or pay packet will probably arrive with the income tax already deducted. This system is called Pay As You Earn, or PAYE.

How do you check the Inland Revenue have done their sums right? First arm yourself with Inland Revenue leaflet **IR22** *Personal Allowances* which sets out the various personal allowances and how much they are worth. Personal allowances are the amounts which you deduct from your earnings to arrive at the amount of money which the Inland Revenue will actually want to tax. These allowances are changed each year in the Budget so you do need to have the up-to-date figures.

## Personal allowances

Everyone is entitled to at least one tax allowance. This is what you were entitled to claim during the 1988-89 tax year.

- The single person's allowance is £2,605. Everyone who isn't married gets this allowance.
- The married man's allowance is £4,095. Any married man can claim this allowance. It is worth more than the single person's allowance. It can be transferred to a married woman if she is working but her husband isn't.
- The wife's earned income allowance is £2,605. Working wives claim this allowance. It is worth the same as the single person's allowance. It can only be set against earned income, not investment income. For tax purposes the Inland Revenue treats a wife's income from her savings and investments as belonging to her husband.
- Additional personal allowance is £1,490. This allowance brings the single person's allowance up to the level of the married man's allowance. Single parents who look after or have financial responsibility for a child can claim this allowance in addition to their single person's allowance. A married man whose wife is totally incapacitated for the whole of the tax year can also claim this additional allowance.
- Widow's bereavement allowance is £1,490. An additional tax allowance which a widow can claim in the tax year of her husband's death, and the following year.
- Age allowance. The old age pensioner's allowance. There are two levels of age allowance: the basic allowance which anyone can claim from the tax year they reach 65, and a slightly higher one for those aged 80 and over. For single people aged between 65 and 79 the allowance is £3,180, rising to £3,310 for those over 80. For married couples aged between 65 and 79, the allowance is £5,035, rising to £5,205 for those 80 and over.
- Blind person's allowance is £540. Any registered blind person can claim this allowance.

THE INLAND REVENUE

## HOW TO CHOOSE YOUR ACCOUNTANT...

*You will require a comprehensive and caring service which could include...*

● Accounts preparation ● Taxation planning and advice ● New business presentation ● Book keeping and VAT ● Computer services ● Company formation and secretarial services ● Auditing ● Management and financial service ● Trust administration ● Trust administration ● Management buyouts ● Corporate finance.

Established for over one hundred years, we have developed the organization to provide these services.

*Our business is to serve your business*

Holland House    1 Oakfield, Sale, Cheshire      061-905 1616
55-57 Flixton Road    Urmston, Manchester      061-748 1121

---

*FOR SUCCESS IN BUSINESS, CALL IN THE PROFESSIONALS*

# HURST & COMPANY
## CHARTERED ACCOUNTANTS

| MANAGEMENT BUYOUTS | MANAGEMENT ACCOUNTS |
| CAPITAL RAISING | BUSINESS PLANS |
| TAX CONSULTANCY | AUDITING |
| BUSINESS ACQUISITION | NEW BUSINESS START |
| ADVICE | ADVICE |

16 Station Road, Cheadle Hulme, Cheshire SK8 5AE
Tel: 061-486 9419/485 8617

Stamford House, Northenden Road, Sale, Cheshire M33 2DH
Tel: 061-962 0048

MANAGING YOUR MONEY

## PENDRAGON FINANCIAL SERVICES

22 BUGDENS LANE
VERWOOD, DORSET.
TEL. (0202) 827010

### Independent and Specialist advisers in matters of Taxation and Financial Planning

- Tax compliance service • Inheritance Tax Planning •
- Capital and Regular Investments • School Fees •
- Life Assurance • Mortgages • Pensions •
- Accountancy service available •

### Checking your Notice of Coding

If you work for an employer and keep the financial clutter down to a minimum, you may not see a tax return from one year to the next. For you, the most important document is your *Notice of Coding*. If you do feel the need to fill in a tax return, you can always ask for one. It's up to you to tell the Inland Revenue if you have a source of income which should be taxed. It's no excuse to say they should have sent you a tax return.

The calendar year runs from January to December. The same is not true of the tax year. This begins on 6 April in one year, and ends on 5 April the following year.

The Inland Revenue send you a Notice of Coding every March. This sets out your tax code, which your employer uses to work out how much tax to deduct from your pay under PAYE. If your tax code is correct, you will end up paying the right amount of tax, give or take a couple of pounds.

For some reason, known only to the Inland Revenue, Notices of Coding are sent out in March for the following tax year. This is usually before the Budget which sets the level of personal allowances, so at this stage your Notice of Coding isn't accurate. However, you can tell if the Inland Revenue have given you the correct allowances, and your employer will adjust your code after any Budget changes.

Your actual tax code is normally a three-digit number followed by a letter. The number is the sum of all your allowances and outgoings divided by 10. If they add up to £2,500, for example, your code is 250.

The letter tells your employer which allowance you are getting. The letter 'L' after the number stands for LOWER and refers to the single person's or wife's earned income allowance; 'H' stands for HIGHER and the married man's allowance or the additional personal allowance; 'P' is for the single person's age allowance; 'V' is for the married man's age allowance. If you don't want your employer to know about your allowances, you can ask your tax office to use the letter 'T' in your code.

Your tax code is not only affected by your personal allowances. There are other factors, known as *outgoings*, which can have a bearing on your Notice of Coding.

If you have a mortgage you can claim tax relief on some or all of the interest payments.

These days most people are in the Mortgage Interest Relief at Source (MIRAS) scheme. See Chapter 9, *Buying a Home*, for a full explanation of MIRAS. With MIRAS your mortgage payments are reduced by an amount equal to the tax relief. If you are in the MIRAS scheme, mortgage interest relief no longer forms part of your Notice of Coding, unless you pay higher-rate tax.

There are still some people whose mortgages aren't covered by the MIRAS scheme. If you have a mortgage of more than £30,000 which you took out before April 1987, you may need to claim the tax relief directly from the Inland Revenue, in which case get it put on your Notice of Coding.

Other outgoings include allowable expenses – money you spend while doing your job. If you are an employee don't expect to get away with much. If you use your car in your job, you might try claiming part of the expense of running it. Driving to and from work doesn't count. If special clothes, tools, or instruments are necessary in your line of work, try claiming for these. Fees to a professional body are also allowable.

All these outgoings increase your coding, the effect of which is to reduce your tax bill each week or month.

But it also works the other way. If you receive regular interest payments which are not taxed before you get them, the Inland Revenue may try to collect the tax through your pay packet. This applies in particular to income from National Savings Ordinary and

Investment accounts which still pay interest with no tax taken away at source.

Figure 2.1 shows a typical Notice of Coding for the tax year 1988–89. In this case, our taxpayer is a single person, entitled to a single person's allowance of £2,425. (Note that the allowance given in the Notice of Coding is for the previous tax year. This is because Notices of Codings are normally sent out before the Budget. They are adjusted automatically once the new personal allowances are known.)

In the previous tax year his Post Office Investment account earned interest of £100, which the Inland Revenue decide to tax through his pay packet. His allowances come to £2,425. But after deducting the £100 interest which he received, the total is reduced to £2,325. This gives a tax code of 232L.

## Checking your tax bill

If your tax code is correct you are likely to be paying the right amount of tax. But how do you check it?

If you are a basic-rate taxpayer and you haven't got a tax return, the best time to check your tax bill is when your employer sends you your P60 soon after the end of the tax year.

The first step is working out your total income. Don't be surprised if the figure for income on your P60 doesn't tally with what you thought you earned that year. You don't pay tax on any contributions to your company pension scheme, and your employer deducts these before arriving at a figure for income.

To get to a final figure for income, you must add up all your sources of income. You may have earnings from a second job, or occasional freelance work. You must add on any income from savings or investments where no tax has been taken off. The most usual sources of untaxed investment income are National Savings Ordinary and Investment accounts, and government stocks bought through the post office.

The second step is working out your allowances and outgoings. The biggest single item is likely to be your personal tax allowance.

If you pay your mortgage through the MIRAS system simply leave it out of the calculation. Outgoings include allowable business expenses, and subscriptions to professional organisations.

Step three: deduct your allowances and outgoings from your total income.

Step four: you now have a figure for taxable income. This is the amount which the Inland Revenue tax. To find out how much,

THE INLAND REVENUE

**Inland Revenue PAYE**

```
644/MT 7890
JP | 13 | 12 | 11 | P
```
Please use this reference if you write or call.
It will help to avoid delay.

MISS V. ORDINARY
6 NOWHERE STREET
ANY TOWN

District date stamp

TAXALL DISTRICT
INSPECTOR HOUSE
INCOME STREET
CAPITAL-ON-SEA

### Notice of coding year to 5 April 1989

This notice cancels any previous notice of coding for the year shown above. It shows the allowances which make up your code. Your employer or paying officer will use this code to deduct or refund the right amount of tax under PAYE during the year shown above.

Please check this notice. If you think it is wrong please return it to me and give your reasons. If we cannot agree you have the right of appeal.

Please let me know at once about any change in your personal circumstances which may alter your allowances and coding.

| See Note | Allowances | £ | See Note | Less Deductions | £ |
|---|---|---|---|---|---|
| 11 | Expenses ... ... ... | | 25 | State pension/benefits | |
| 17 | Age (estimated income £............) | | 25 | Occupational pension | |
| | | | 25 | Untaxed interest ... | 100 |
| 17 | Personal ... ... ... | 2,425 | 29 | Tax unpaid £ ............... | |
| 17 | Wife's earned income | | | | |
| | | | | Less total deductions | 100 |
| | Total allowances ... | 2,425 | | Allowances set against pay etc. £ | 2,325 |

Please keep this notice for future reference and let me know of any change in your address.
**See Form P3(T) enclosed or previously sent.**

Your code for the year to 5 April 198  is  233 L    see Part  A  overleaf

**P2(T)(MAN)**

**Figure 2.1** Notice of Coding

simply apply the basic rate of tax to the figure for taxable income.

If your Notice of Coding didn't include all the allowances and outgoings to which you are entitled, then the Inland Revenue owe you money. On the other hand, if you have income which the Inland Revenue doesn't know about, you will owe them money. In these circumstances, ask for a tax return. Don't try avoiding the tax, they catch up with you in the end, and paying one year's tax is easier than paying six.

Here's how one family checked their tax bill against their P60, for the 1987-88 tax year.

The husband's P60 showed an income of £12,500, and that he paid income tax of £2,350. He was entitled to claim a married man's personal allowance of £3,795 and his subscription of £100 to his professional organisation. His allowances and outgoings came to £3,895.

He deducted this from his total income of £12,500 and arrived at a taxable income of £8,605 on which his tax bill is calculated.

The basic rate of tax stood at 27 per cent in the 1987-88 tax year. His tax bill is 27 per cent of £8,605 which works out at £2,323. This is £27 less than the tax deducted at source from his pay packet and shown on his P60.

It looks as if he forgot to tell the Inland Revenue about his subscription to his professional body and it was not allowed for in his Notice of Coding. He now writes to his tax inspector claiming a rebate, and asking for his current Notice of Coding to be adjusted.

## How much tax do I pay?

Income tax is always expressed as a percentage. Most people pay what is called *Basic Rate Tax*.

The basic rate of tax is fixed at the Budget. In recent years it has come down from an all-time high of 35 per cent in the two years between 1975 and 1977 to 25 per cent in the 1988-89 tax year. This doesn't mean that if you earn £10,000 a year you pay the full 25 per cent to the Inland Revenue. Most people find they pay less because they only pay tax on the amount which is left after they have deducted their outgoings and personal allowances.

Only the wealthy pay more. If you earn above a certain level you pay *higher rate tax* of 40 per cent on the top slice of your income. In the 1988-89 tax year, you pay higher rate tax on any taxable income over £19,300. So if your taxable income, after deducting all allowances and outgoings is £25,000, you pay basic rate tax of 25 per cent on the first £19,300, and 40 per cent on the remaining £5,700. You don't pay 40 per cent on the entire £25,000.

---

# McCaffrey & Co.
## CHARTERED ACCOUNTANTS

23a University Road
Belfast
Co. Antrim BT7 1NA

Telephone: Belfast (0232) 249518

---

**Working for yourself**

If you work for yourself, you won't pay your income tax through the PAYE system and you can legitimately get away with paying your tax nearly two years later than everyone else. But you have to pay it in the end, so if you are self-employed don't live to the limit of your income. Always remember the tax inspector will want his cut eventually.

The Inland Revenue looks favourably on those who work for themselves. So if you have the chance to go self-employed or can line up some freelance work, grab it.

If you are self-employed you only pay tax on the profit you make from running your business. To work out your profit you add up your income and deduct all your business expenses.

These include the obvious things like the cost of the materials you use in your business, stationery, travel, rent and secretarial help. But there are also the less obvious expenses, many of which you can't normally claim if you work for someone else.

For example, if you are self-employed and work at home at least some of the time you can claim:

MANAGING YOUR MONEY

# P60 Certificate of pay, Income Tax and National Insurance Contributions

DO NOT DESTROY

| Employee's National Insurance number | | | | | Enter here<br>"M" if male<br>"F" if female | | | Tax District and reference | | Year to<br>5 April |

Employee's surname in CAPITAL letters — First two forenames

Employer's full name and address

### National Insurance contributions in this employment

| Contribution Table letter | Earnings on which employee's contributions payable (Whole £s only) 1a | Total of Employee's and Employer's contributions payable 1b | Employee's contributions payable 1c | Earnings on which employee's contributions at Contracted-out rate payable included in 1a (Whole £s only) 1d | Employee's contributions at Contracted-out rate included in 1c 1e |

Employee's works/payroll number etc.

Employee's private address

| Statutory Sick Pay | Statutory Maternity Pay |

Amounts included in the "Pay" section of the "This employment" box below ▶

| Total for year | | Previous employment | | This employment | |
| Pay | Tax deducted | Pay | Tax deducted | Pay | Tax deducted or refunded (R) |

Complete only for occupational pension schemes newly contracted-out since 1 January 1986:
Scheme contracted-out number

**S 4**

Final tax code

| Employee's Widows & Orphans/life insurance contributions in this employment | Week 53 Payment indicator |

This certificate shows the total amount of pay for income tax purposes that I/we have paid to you in the year. Any overtime, bonus, commission etc. is included. It also gives details of the total tax and National Insurance contributions deducted by me/us (less any refunds) in the year.
**To the employee:** Please keep this certificate in a safe place as you will not be able to get a duplicate. It will help you check any Notice of Assessment that the Tax Office may send you. You can also use it to check that your employer is deducting the right type of National Insurance contributions for you and using your correct National Insurance number. If he is not please tell him.

Sprocket margins to be removed and forms cleanly separated before sending to Inspector of Taxes

P60 substitute (SCB 1) 3 PART

26

## "IT ALL ADDS UP – TO WHY YOU CHOOSE US"

### SERVICE
- Professional service with personal touch
- Expertise in all aspects of business and personal tax and business problems

### EXPERTISE
- Fully qualified
- Highly trained
- Grants, Taxation
- Business advice Limited Companies Raising Finance Costing & Much More

### LOCAL KNOWLEDGE
- 4 Local offices
- Continuity of dealing with same person
- Local knowledge of conditions
- Quality staff you know and can trust

### MOORE BEDWORTH & CO.

**BARNSTAPLE**
45131 Alliance House
Cross Street

**ILFRACOMBE**
62498 96 High Street

**BIDEFORD**
720171 80 High Street

**SOUTH MOLTON**
3621 6 The Square

---

# Lacome & Co.
### Chartered Accountants

We offer a personal and professional service to Companies, Partnerships and individuals on all financial and taxation matters.

- AUDITS
- TAXATION
- V.A.T.
- P.A.Y.E.
- BOOK-KEEPING

- RAISING OF FINANCE
- PREPARATION OF ACCOUNTS
- MANAGEMENT CONSULTANCY
- INVESTMENT AND PENSION ADVICE
- COMPANY FORMATIONS

*Just starting up — Need all kinds of advice? We can help*

### TELEPHONE: 01-346 1992
**INITIAL MEETING FREE OF CHARGE**

- a proportion of your household bills: gas, electricity, rent, cleaning, maintenance and repairs.
- all or some of the cost of running your car if you use it for business.

You can claim expenses even if you only work for yourself part-time, or do some occasional freelance work. But remember, if these expenses exceed what you actually earn while working for yourself, you can't then offset them against your PAYE earnings.

The self-employed can also claim *capital allowances*. These are allowances which help you to pay for any big items which you use 'wholly and exclusively' in your business. They could be anything from a car, to a computer, a long-distance lorry, or a sewing machine. You can get a partial capital allowance if you buy things which you use both privately and in your business. You must agree the proportion with your tax inspector.

How do capital allowances work? Say you are claiming a capital allowance on just one item. In the first year you can claim 25 per cent of the cost of the item. In the second and subsequent years, you can claim up to 25 per cent of the item's *written down value*. The written down value decreases year by year and is arrived at by deducting the previous year's capital allowance.

So if you buy a computer for £1,000, your first year's capital allowance is a quarter or £250. Your second year's written down value is £750 (£1,000 less £250) and the capital allowance is 25 per cent of this, which works out at £188.

## The tax return

Has your tax return sunk unopened and unanswered to the bottom of your personal pending tray at the back of some drawer?

Be brave, the tax return is not as daunting as it looks. Most people's tax affairs are simple and straightforward. Most people have nothing worth hiding. So bite on the bullet and fill in the wretched thing. It will probably take you less than an hour.

Tax returns are normally sent out in April, just as the new tax year begins. The tax return is divided into six sections: Earnings; Pensions; Investments, savings etc; Outgoings; Capital Gains and Allowances.

With the exception of the section marked Allowances, the tax people want to know what happened to you in the tax year which has just ended. In the Allowances section they want to know what allowances you are claiming in the tax year just beginning.

The tax return comes in several versions. If your tax life is simple, you will probably be sent Form P1. If it gets more complicated you graduate to Form 11P. The self-employed get Form 11.

If you work for an employer, the Inland Revenue want to know how much you earned. Enter the amount after deducting any payments you made into your company's pension scheme in the line marked 'EARNINGS FROM FULL-TIME EMPLOYMENT'. If you sometimes earn money from another source, especially if tax is deducted under PAYE, enter it on the next line marked 'ALL OTHER EARNINGS'.

If you are self-employed or have substantial part-time or freelance earnings, wait until the next line marked 'PROFITS FROM A TRADE OR PROFESSION' and enter your profits here. Attach a copy of your accounts, detailing your income and your outgoings.

You are liable to income tax on the income you get from your savings and investments. Certain interest payments and most dividend payments arrive with tax at the basic rate already deducted.

Interest from UK banks and building societies and dividends from UK ordinary shares and unit trusts are all paid with an amount for basic-rate tax already taken off. For most people there is no extra tax to pay. But you still need to fill in the amounts on your tax return.

If you have several bank and building society accounts this can be a chore, and you will probably need to list them on a separate sheet of paper. Enter the actual amount of interest you got from bank and building society accounts under the heading 'INTEREST FROM ANY OTHER BANKS AND BUILDING SOCIETIES'.

When you get dividends from shares and unit trusts, they arrive with a *tax voucher*. This shows the dividend and the *tax credit*, which is the amount deducted for tax. Enter both the dividend and the tax credit on the line marked 'COMPANY DIVIDENDS AND UNIT TRUSTS'.

You pay tax on interest which is paid gross with no deduction for tax. National Savings Ordinary and Investment accounts fall into this category, as do government stocks bought at the Post Office through the National Savings Stock Register. Enter interest from National Savings accounts, including National Savings Deposit and Income bonds under the heading 'NATIONAL SAVINGS BANK INTEREST'.

Interest on government stocks bought through the Post Office should be entered later under the heading 'INTEREST NOT ALREADY TAXED FROM ANOTHER SOURCE'.

If you hold government stock or local authority loans bought through a stockbroker, you get your interest net, after tax has been

MANAGING YOUR MONEY

### Investments, savings, etc

If you received income during the year ended 5 April 1986 from any of the sources listed below, please tick the appropriate boxes, enter the annual amounts and give details in the space provided.

| | Self | Wife | Self | Wife | Details |
|---|---|---|---|---|---|
| Rents from land or property | ☐ | ☐ | £ | £ | |
| National Savings Bank interest — Ordinary account | ☐ | ☐ | | | |
| Investment account | ☐ | ☐ | | | |
| Interest from any other banks and building societies | ☐ | ☐ | | | |
| Interest from banks not already taxed | ☐ | ☐ | | | |
| Interest not already taxed from any other source | ☐ | ☐ | | | |
| Income from abroad | ☐ | ☐ | | | |
| Company dividends and unit trusts | ☐ | ☐ | | | |
| Other dividends, interest, etc, including income from trusts | ☐ | ☐ | | | |
| Payments from settlements and estates (gross amount) | ☐ | ☐ | | | |
| Maintenance, alimony or aliment received (gross amount) | ☐ | ☐ | | | |
| Any other income or gains | ☐ | ☐ | | | |

Remember to read the notes 'How to fill in your tax return' as you complete each section.

### Outgoings

If you wish to claim for a tax deduction or any allowable payment which you made in the year ended 5 April 1986, please tick the appropriate boxes, enter the amounts paid in the year and give details in the space provided.

| | Self | Wife | Self | Wife | Details |
|---|---|---|---|---|---|
| Expenses paid in connection with your work | ☐ | ☐ | £ | £ | |
| Subscriptions to professional bodies | ☐ | ☐ | | | |
| Interest on loans for buying or improving your home | ☐ | ☐ | | | |
| Interest payments on property for letting | ☐ | ☐ | | | |
| Number of weeks let _____ | | | | | |
| Other loan interest paid | ☐ | ☐ | | | |
| Covenants | ☐ | ☐ | | | |
| Maintenance, alimony or aliment paid | ☐ | ☐ | | | |
| Rents and yearly interest paid to persons abroad | ☐ | ☐ | | | |

**Figure 2.3** The tax return (specimen page from P1)

taken off. Get the gross figure off the tax voucher and enter it under the heading 'OTHER DIVIDENDS, INTEREST, ETC, INCLUDING INCOME FROM TRUSTS'.

You don't need to tell the taxman about tax-free interest payments, such as Save As You Earn and National Savings Certificates.

## How to appeal

If the Inland Revenue send you a tax bill, and you think they have got their sums wrong, you have the right to appeal. You must do this within 30 days of receiving your *Notice of Assessment*. This is the document which explains how your tax bill is worked out. If you are self-employed you must also apply to postpone payment of the tax, and give your reasons why you think the Inland Revenue have made a mistake. Again, you must do this within 30 days of getting the Notice of Assessment.

Having appealed you now argue your case out with your tax office. If you fail to agree you can take it to the General or Special Commissioners. The *General Commissioners* are panels of local worthies. The *Special Commissioners* are the real tax experts. You won't always be free to choose where your appeal is heard.

## Tax and marriage

The dress, the flowers, the speech, whether or not to ask great-aunt Ada. These are the important things to worry about when you get married.

But don't wait too long to share your happy news with the Inland Revenue – it could save you money. The government is introducing a new separate taxation system for married couples from April 1990, but for the time being, it remains a fact that when you marry your tax position changes, and the Inland Revenue need to know if they are to get your tax right.

There are extra tax allowances to claim, and most people pay less tax once they are married.

High-earning couples are the exception. If they forget to tell the Inland Revenue the consequence is a hefty demand for extra tax.

Whatever you think of each other, the tax people think of married couples as one, but a one in which men and women aren't equal. If both of you work, your tax bill is calculated on your joint incomes. Surprisingly, most couples do end up paying less tax. But it's the husband who gets the benefit in his pay packet, not the wife.

This is because the husband now claims the higher married man's personal allowance, instead of the lower single person's allowance. Wives exchange their single person's allowance for the wife's earned income allowance. But as this is set at the same level as the single person's allowance, they get no direct tax benefit from being married.

As things stand at the moment, the tax system stops people from getting married. High-flying couples, where both partners earn big salaries, are better off financially staying single and living together.

If you stay single you can buy a house together and get tax relief on a mortgage of up to £60,000, each person claiming the maximum of £30,000. Once you marry the tax relief on your mortgage is limited to £30,000. The 1988 Budget has put a stop to what is effectively a tax on marriage. From August 1988, mortgage interest tax relief is to be restricted to £30,000 for each house or flat, rather than each single person.

If you decide to get married but forget to tell your tax office, you may end up paying a lot of extra tax. You will have to repay the mortgage interest relief above £30,000. You may also find when you add your two incomes together it pushes you into a much higher tax bracket and there is a bill for higher-rate tax.

There is no way of getting extra tax relief on your mortgage other than by getting a divorce, and anyway this ploy no longer works after August 1988. But you can avoid paying higher-rate tax on your joint incomes.

To do this you must make what is called *The wife's earned income election*. Ask the Inland Revenue for form 14-1. This way, your earnings are taxed separately, as if you were two single people again. The husband loses his married man's allowance and returns to the position before he was married, claiming the single person's allowances.

If your joint incomes only just push you into higher-rate tax, you may still be better off being taxed together and continuing to get the married man's personal allowance.

Separate taxation doesn't apply to investments, and any income from these is taxed jointly.

Married couples can also opt for separate assessment. This doesn't reduce your tax bill. It just allocates the allowances in proportion to the amount each person earns. For separate assessment ask the Inland Revenue for form 11S.

There is one additional quirk. If the tax system encourages wealthy couples to stay single, it also gives men a financial incentive to stay at home and send their wives out to work. A working wife can claim the married man's allowance in addition to her own, when her husband isn't earning. The same is not true for men whose wives stay at home; they aren't entitled to claim the wife's earned income allowance.

But there is still one note of inequality under the new system. So that men don't find themselves paying more tax, a new allowance called the married couple's allowance is to be introduced. This is an additional allowance which makes up the difference between the new personal allowance and the old married man's allowance. The new married couple's allowance goes to the husband, although it can be transferred to the wife if the husband doesn't earn enough to claim all or part of it. There is currently no proposal for men and women to automatically share this new allowance.

# 3
# WHERE TO KEEP YOUR CASH

Opening your first bank account, getting your first cheque book and writing your first cheque, are some of those little initiations into the adult world which few of us ever forget.

But we are also walking into a world full of pitfalls and hidden dangers, which, unless we are fully prepared, can colour our attitudes towards banks and bankers for the rest of our lives.

Getting to love your bank starts with getting to know what you can and can't do with your bank account. The first lesson is usually learned the hard way. Bank accounts are not a passport to easy living and instant credit. You can't expect to let your account go into the red without getting a letter from your bank manager.

## Bank current accounts

Most people start their love-hate relationship with their bank the day they open a current account. This is the account which comes with a cheque book and paying-in book.

Armed with a *cheque book* you can pay your bills, buy things in shops, and give money to friends. All you do is write out a cheque. You also use a cheque each time you want to get cash out of your bank account.

There are two types of cheque – they can either be *uncrossed* or *crossed*. Unless you specifically ask for uncrossed cheques you will be given crossed cheques. As the name implies a crossed cheque has two lines drawn across it.

A crossed cheque is safer than an uncrossed cheque. When you write someone an uncrossed cheque they can take it to your bank branch and get cash. An uncrossed cheque is known as an open cheque and the dangers are obvious. If that cheque is lost or stolen, someone who has no right to the money can cash it.

When you write someone a crossed cheque, they can normally only cash it by paying it into a bank or savings account. The one exception to this is when you want to get cash out of your own bank account when you can use a crossed cheque.

If you have an uncrossed cheque you can transform it into a crossed cheque just by drawing two lines across it.

FINDING YOUR WAY ROUND YOUR CHEQUE BOOK

Take a look at a cheque. What is the meaning of all those computer hieroglyphics? Start at the top left-hand corner. Here you find the name of your bank, and the address of the branch where your account is held.

Opposite this in the top right-hand corner is the space for writing in the date. Under this, there are six figures broken up with two dashes. This is your bank branch's own sorting code. You will sometimes be asked for this information when you fill in a banker's order form or a paying-in slip (see below).

Below this is the line marked 'Pay'. Here you write the word 'Cash' if you want to get money out of your own bank account, or the name of the shop or person to whom you are paying the cheque.

Underneath are the lines where you enter the amount in words. If it's for a round number of pounds you enter the amount plus the word 'only' and complete the line with a long dash.

If the amount is for pounds and pence, spell out the pounds in words, but write the pence in numbers. Once again complete the line with a long dash. Any amount less than 10 pence, should be prefixed with a '0'; so 6p is written as '06p', and 3p as '03p'.

Opposite there is the box where you enter the value of the cheque in numbers. The name of the account holder is printed below the box.

Running along the bottom of your cheque is a row of computer numbers which are not always easy to decipher. Reading from the left, the first set is the cheque number, which runs in sequence from cheque to cheque. The same number appears on the cheque stub, if there is one. The next sequence is your branch code, while the last spells out your account number.

Always fill in your cheque stubs. You may think you can remember how much money you spend, but it's easy to make mistakes, and without the record on your cheque stubs, you can't

MANAGING YOUR MONEY

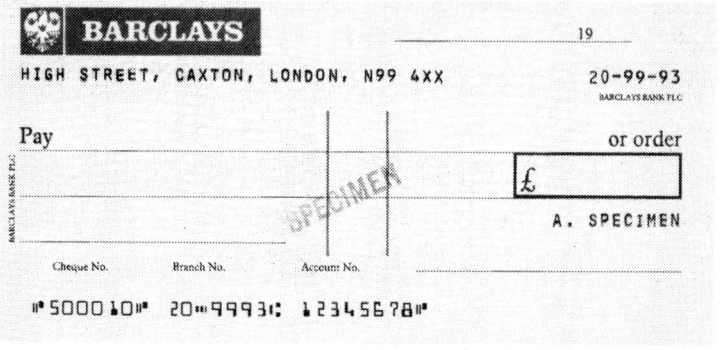

**Figure 3.1** Cheques

check your bank statement when it comes in. If you do lose track though, all is not lost. Banks don't automatically return cheques but you do have the right to ask for them.

Keep a record of your account number separately from your cheque book or cheque guarantee card, just in case they get stolen or lost and you need to tell your bank quickly.

PAYING MONEY INTO YOUR BANK ACCOUNT

When you want to put money into your account, whether it's cash or cheques, you can either use your own paying-in book or a paying-in slip which you pick up at the bank. Your paying-in book is personal to you. The paying-in slip isn't so you have to fill in your account number and the bank's sorting code.

When you pay cash into your account, you can draw it out again immediately. When you pay in a cheque, on the other hand, you have to wait at least three working days for the cheque to clear before you can take it out.

Remember there is no fee if you pay money into your account at any branch of your own bank, but there often is if you use any other bank.

BANK STATEMENTS

If you have the standard type of cheque account with one of the high street clearing banks, your statements never seem to bring good news. Even if you try to keep track of your finances, the final figure never seems to tally with what's on your statement.

It's partly because statements arrive so infrequently, usually four times a year (although you can ask for them to be sent monthly), and partly because of the workings of the clearing system.

With this type of account which offers free banking so long as your account stays in credit, you can find yourself paying bank charges even though your bank statement appears to have been continuously in credit. This is because your bank statement shows what is known as the ledger balance, but bank charges are levied on what is known as the cleared balance. Any cheques which you pay into your bank account appear on your ledger immediately, but they don't turn up on your cleared balance for at least three working days, when the cheque has been cleared. So you can go into the red while you are waiting for a cheque to be cleared, and end up paying bank charges, even though your bank statement shows you to have been continuously in credit.

MANAGING YOUR MONEY

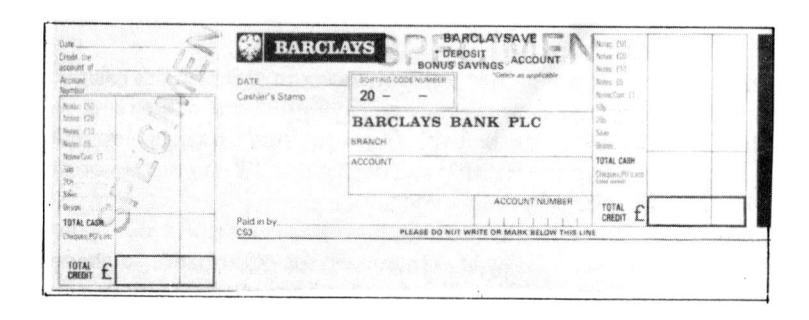

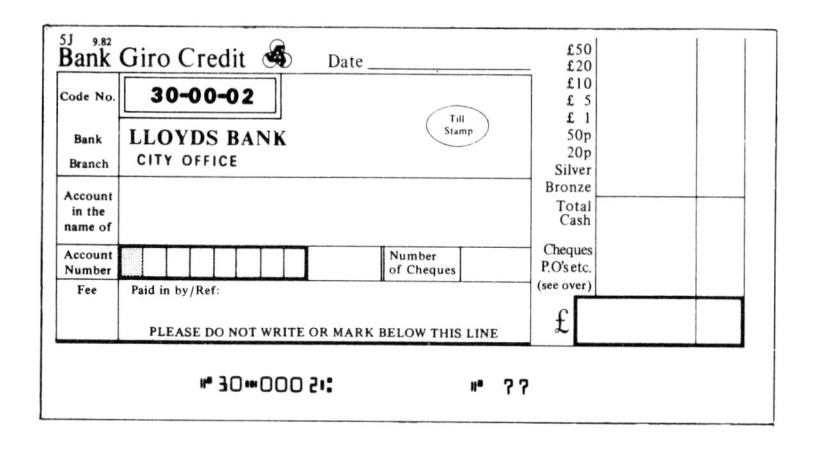

**Figure 3.2** Paying-in slips

WHERE TO KEEP YOUR CASH

MR VR ORDINARY
**PROVINCIAL BANK**
32-36 MARKET PLACE
ANYTOWN TEL 0123 45 678
5898   MR VICTOR ORDINARY
G037   6 NOWHERE STREET
0329   ANY TOWN
1/2

3470
CHEQUE
**STATEMENT OF ACCOUNT**

DIARY
8JAN88

POST   NO.   10

| DETAILS | PAYMENTS | RECEIPTS | DATE | BALANCE |
|---|---|---|---|---|
|  |  |  | 1987 |  |
| BALANCE FORWARD |  |  | 7NOV | 869.37 |
| 200220 | 31.45 |  | 10NOV | 837.92 |
| 200221 | 36.95 |  | 12NOV |  |
| 200222 | 50.00 |  | 12NOV | 750.97 |
| CASH 180631   13NOV |  |  |  |  |
| WELLING BROADWAY1 | 50.00 |  | 14NOV | 700.97 |
| CASH 180631   19NOV |  |  |  |  |
| WELLING BROADWAY1 | 50.00 |  | 19NOV | 650.97 |
| A N B S |  |  |  |  |
| WY 20666 ORD   STO | 100.00 |  | 21NOV | 550.97 |
| 200223 | 34.17 |  | 25NOV | 516.80 |
| CASH 180631   26NOV |  |  |  |  |
| WELLING BROADWAY2 | 50.00 |  | 27NOV |  |
| PASCAL GREEN   BGC |  | 646.72 | 27NOV | 1113.52 |
| 200224 | 67.94 |  | 2DEC | 1045.58 |
| 200225 | 43.06 |  | 3DEC |  |
| 200227 | 12.79 |  | 3DEC | 989.73 |
| ABBEY NAT B/SOC |  |  |  |  |
| RWY3 297/ORD   STO | 10.00 |  | 5DEC |  |
| CASH 180631 4DEC |  |  |  |  |
| WELLING BROADWAY2 | 50.00 |  | 5DEC | 929.73 |
| LBW DATA RATES |  |  |  |  |
| 2513042   STO | 23.30 |  | 8DEC | 906.43 |
| 200226 | 50.00 |  | 9DEC |  |
| 200228 | 29.99 |  | 9DEC | 826.44 |
| CASH 180631 12DEC |  |  |  |  |
| WELLING BROADWAY2 | 50.00 |  | 12DEC | 776.44 |
| 200231 | 7.99 |  | 16DEC |  |
| 200232 | 10.43 |  | 16DEC | 758.02 |
| 200230 | 43.77 |  | 17DEC |  |
| CASH 180631 17DEC |  |  |  |  |
| WELLING BROADWAY2 | 100.00 |  | 17DEC | 614.25 |
| PASCAL GREEN   BGC |  | 806.82 | 18DEC | 1421.07 |
| 200229 | 62.00 |  | 22DEC |  |
| 200233 | 7.20 |  | 22DEC |  |
| 200234 | 6.90 |  | 22DEC | 1344.97 |

ABBREVIATIONS:   DIV Dividend   STO Standing Order   BGC Bank Giro Credit   DDR Direct Debit   DR Overdrawn Balances

**Figure 3.3** Bank statement

# MANAGING YOUR MONEY

Keeping a very firm grip on how much you have in your bank account is one way to avoid overdrawing by mistake. The other is to ask your bank manager to send you statements once a month.

### THE CHEQUE GUARANTEE CARD

A cheque guarantee card guarantees that any cheque you write for less than £50 won't be bounced by the bank, but see below, *Writing big cheques*. Many shops don't accept cheques unless they are backed by a cheque guarantee card.

Most first-time bank customers find it all too easy to open a bank account. But then find they can't use it to the full because the bank manager won't give them a bank guarantee card.

It's Catch 22: the bank manager says he wants to see how you handle your account before he lets you loose with a guarantee card. But you can't prove you can use your account responsibly until you have a card.

Most people find they have to wait three to six months before they get a cheque guarantee card. The exception is Barclays, where the Barclaycard credit card also acts as a cheque guarantee card. Anyone can apply for a Barclaycard, and you can apply for one as soon as you open an account with Barclays. It is then up to Barclaycard whether they give you one.

Students are often given cheque guarantee cards when they open an account. The banks see today's students as tomorrow's wealthy customers and fall over themselves to sign them up. Students usually find they can get a cheque guarantee card along with their first grant cheque.

**Figure 3.4** Cheque guarantee card

WRITING BIG CHEQUES

When you write a cheque for more than £50, most shops ask you to write your address on the back of the cheque.

Others ask you to go through a little subterfuge. They ask you to write several cheques, all for amounts under £50. The banks dislike the ploy, and say they bounce cheques if they think this is what you have done and your account goes into the red. But it can be difficult to prove if the shop asks you to put different dates on the cheques.

If you want to pay strictly by the rule book it is often quickest and cheapest to withdraw the money in cash from your bank account.

If the idea of carrying around a large amount of cash fills you with foreboding, use a *credit card* (see page 43).

You can't do this if you don't have a credit card or your credit limit is too low. But there are still a couple of ways round the problem if you don't mind paying the bank charges involved.

You can write out a cheque and the shop can take it to their bank and ask for *special clearance*. The cheque will be cleared the next day and you can collect whatever you bought. The shop normally asks you to pay any special clearance fee.

You can ask your bank for a *banker's draft*. This is as good as cash, but often takes several days to come through and costs a few pounds.

GETTING CASH

You can cash cheques up to any amount at your own bank branch, so long as the money is in your account. If you have a cheque guarantee card, you can use this to draw cash from other branches of your bank. You can also use your cheque guarantee card in other banks if you don't mind paying a small fee.

If your own bank branch isn't convenient, it's often a good idea to ask for an *open credit* with the branch nearest your home or work. The bank usually charges for arranging an open credit, but once you have it, you have the facility to cash cheques at another branch up to an agreed limit with no questions asked.

It is now possible to withdraw cash from your bank account outside banking hours. Ask your bank for a cash dispenser card. It's a small plastic card, looking much like a credit card, which allows you to get cash out of one of your bank's cash dispensers.

PAYING BILLS BY CHEQUE

When you pay a bill by cheque you can deliver it by hand, post it, or pay it through a bank *giro* form. Most everyday bills for the telephone, gas and electricity come with a bank giro form. Use this form with a cheque and you can pay your bills over the bank counter, and save the postage or shoe leather, although there is a charge if you use a bank other than your own.

### STANDING ORDERS AND DIRECT DEBITS

Cheques are not the only way to pay money to other people. Standing orders and direct debits are the best way of making regular payments. With these you tell your bank that you want to pay for something by regular, usually monthly, payments. The money is then automatically taken from your account on the day you specify without your having to do anything.

A *standing order* is entirely under your control. The amount you pay under a standing order cannot be altered without a written instruction from you.

A *direct debit* is different. With a direct debit, you give someone direct access to your account for a specific amount of money. In theory they can ask for any amount they like. In practice most reputable organisations inform you when they intend to increase the direct debit.

Standing orders are used to pay for things such as mortgage repayments, rates and savings schemes, while direct debits are used for things like magazine subscriptions or National Insurance contributions where the amount changes fairly frequently.

### STOPPING A CHEQUE

If you write a cheque and then change your mind, or the cheque is lost, you can often stop the cheque going through if you let your bank know before the cheque is cleared. Your bank will want you to write and confirm it, and they charge you for the service. But remember you can't stop a cheque which is backed by a cheque guarantee card.

### CASH DISPENSERS

Banks are rarely open when you need them. They open their doors after you leave for work, and close just as you find time to dash off for a late lunch. And, with the exception of the few bank branches which are open on Saturday morning, most are locked and barred on the busiest shopping day of the week. There is no doubt that banking hours are infuriatingly inconvenient, which is why the banks put in cash dispensers, operated with a plastic card.

Even if there isn't a cash dispenser near where you live or work, a cash dispenser card is well worth having. You can use it anywhere in this country. And you can often use it in other banks' cash dispensers. When you get your card, you are given a weekly limit.

This is the amount you can withdraw each week through a cash dispenser. You can go up to this limit provided your account is not overdrawn. The simplest machines just hand you the money and give you a balance. Others allow you to order cheque books and statements, and pay in money.

When you use a cash dispenser you key in a secret code number – called a *Personal Identification Number*, PIN for short – which you should memorise. You won't find this number anywhere on the card. If you can't remember it, keep a note of it totally separately from your card. Otherwise you may be giving a thief the key which opens your bank account.

## Credit cards

If your idea of heaven is a little plastic wallet full of plastic cards, the best place to start is your bank. Barclays, the Trustee Savings Bank, the National Girobank and the Bank of Scotland issue the blue, white and gold Visa card; Lloyds, Midland, National Westminster and the Royal Bank of Scotland issue the green, white and red Access card.

The banks tend to keep their credit card operation separate from their other activities and you can apply for a credit card from a bank where you don't have an account. Most people ask their own bank first. But if you bank with Barclays, and have a Visa card, there is nothing to stop you applying for an Access card through, say, the National Westminster.

Barclaycard (Barclays Visa card) is unlike any of the others. As we have already seen, it is more than just a credit card. If you bank with

**Figure 3.5** Access credit card

Barclays Bank it acts as a cheque guarantee card as well.

Apart from this, Visa and Access work in much the same way. You have a credit limit which is the amount you can borrow at any one time. It can be as low as £100, although at Barclaycard the average credit limit at the end of 1987 was £895. If you go over your credit limit you risk losing your card.

Bank credit cards are a good deal if you clear the account each month. This way, if you time your shopping right, you get up to 56 days' free credit.

Some bank credit cards also come with their own PIN number and can be used to get cash advances from cash dispensers.

For a detailed explanation of how bank credit cards work, and how they differ, see Chapter 6, *Borrowing Money*.

## The cost of running a bank current account

How much does it cost to run a bank account? That depends on you and how careful you are. It also depends on what type of bank account you choose. The choice today is much wider than it was just two years ago.

You can opt for:

- An ordinary cheque account with one of the big high street clearing banks.
- An interest-paying cheque account available from some building societies and banks.
- A high-interest cheque account available from some banks and financial services companies.
- A National Girobank cheque account.

All these accounts offer you the basics of a cheque book, cheque guarantee card, and the opportunity to take out a credit card. Where they differ is in the way they levy their charges.

*A clearing bank cheque account*
Most banks now offer what they call *free banking* if you keep your account in the black.

But once you step over that line into the red, even if it is just for a day or so, your bank manager starts charging you for everything in sight, for the whole of that charging period, which for most banks lasts for three months. And to add insult to injury there are interest charges to pay on the overdraft.

When you overdraw you are charged each time you take money

out of your account, whether it is by cheque, standing order, or direct debit. A few banks even charge you for paying in money as well.

Others charge an account maintenance fee. There may even be a charge for sending you a warning letter, additional statements and for arranging an overdraft.

The interest rate on the actual overdraft varies. If you haven't arranged an overdraft with your bank manager you pay a much higher rate of interest than if you have an arranged overdraft.

The only way to avoid paying bank charges (but not interest) when you overdraw is to keep an average balance of at least £500 in your account if you bank with Barclays, Lloyds, or NatWest, or only overdraw for two days if you bank with Midland.

Some banks operate what are known as *convenience limits*. This is the secret figure up to which they allow you to overdraw before they send you a warning letter. Some banks are formalising their convenience limits. Customers are offered an automatic overdraft up to their convenience limit at a rate of interest pitched half way between an arranged and an unarranged overdraft.

This type of bank account offers moderately good value for money if you know you will never need to overdraw. If you need to go into the red occasionally think about a different type of account. Or choose Lloyds Bank which is the only clearing bank to have a monthly, rather than a three monthly charging period.

*An interest-bearing cheque account*
This type of account offers free banking and pays you interest when your account is in credit. The only charge is when you overdraw, when you are charged interest; there are no additional transaction charges when you write a cheque, or make a standing order. These accounts are available from the Abbey National and Nationwide Anglia (Flexaccount) building societies, from HFC Trust and Savings, and from Midland (Vector).

HFC offers the highest rate of interest, but the number of branches is restricted. Midland's Vector account has the disadvantage of charging a £10 a month fee.

Anyone who overdraws occasionally should consider using one of these accounts. The Abbey National and Nationwide Anglia Flexaccount offer the advantage of a large branch network and no charges. The Abbey National even has the first £100 cheque guarantee card.

*A high-interest cheque account*
These accounts start paying interest once the amount in your account goes above a certain amount – often £500. Some accounts

demand a high minimum deposit (between £1,000 and £2,500) to open the account. They are widely available from a number of clearing banks, including the Co-op, Lloyds Bank and the Royal Bank of Scotland; financial services companies, such as Provincial Trust, Save & Prosper and Western Trust and Savings, and the Abbey National Building Society. The terms vary: some offer a free banking service if you remain in credit; others charge a monthly or quarterly service fee; and some make transaction charges; cheque guarantee cards aren't always available. A high-interest cheque account is worth thinking about if you never overdraw and you regularly keep at least £500 in your current account.

*A National Girobank account*
A National Girobank account works much like a clearing bank cheque account, and you have the advantage of being able to cash cheques at over 20,000 post offices.

If you overdraw on your Girobank account, you only get caught for transaction charges while you remain overdrawn. If you regularly overdraw for just a few days, say at the end of the month while you wait for your pay cheque to come through, a Girobank account is definitely worth considering. You can now get an overdraft from the Girobank, but you must apply for one. If you don't have an agreed overdraft you are meant to keep your account in credit although, as mentioned above, they will always give you a couple of days' leeway.

## What else can you do at the bank?

You can save money at your bank, and you can borrow it.

The most popular savings account is a *bank deposit account*. You can open one of these even if you don't have much money to save. Interest is added to your deposit account every six months. To get money out you give the bank seven days' notice. If you need the money more quickly you lose seven days' interest on the amount you take out.

There is not much to be said in favour of bank deposit accounts. The rate of interest is generally lower than on comparable building society accounts. They could provide a useful service if bank managers automatically transferred money from your deposit account to your current account whenever you were in danger of going into the red and wanted to avoid bank charges. Few people can persuade their bank managers to do this.

Nonetheless it is still worth keeping an eye on interest rates. There are times when the banks give a better rate of return than the building societies. And if you have a large amount of money to save, the banks and the buildings societies are usually much of a muchness.

The building societies have always quoted their rates of interest after deducting an amount for basic-rate tax. Since April 1985, the banks have done the same, which makes it easy to compare interest rates. And basic-rate taxpayers don't have any extra tax to pay.

If you want to borrow money, think about an *overdraft*. Borrowing through your cheque account is usually cheaper than using your credit card or taking out hire purchase or borrowing money from a shop.

The cheapest loan is normally an arranged overdraft. To get an arranged overdraft you make a formal request to your bank or building society manager. If your manager agrees an overdraft of, say, £500, your cheque account can go into the red up to £500 without question.

With an overdraft there is no formal agreement to pay the loan off in regular amounts over a number of years. Instead, the manager assesses it every six months, and he can decide to withdraw the facility at a moment's notice.

Before you arrange an overdraft, ask your manager whether he charges an arrangement fee. Some banks do, so if you only want a small overdraft the arrangement fee may make it more expensive than other forms of borrowing.

Also remember that on clearing bank cheque accounts you are charged bank charges when you are overdrawn. So write as few cheques as possible, and buy everything on a credit card, and pay it off with a cheque once a month.

If your manager doesn't want to give you an overdraft he may let you take out a *personal loan*. They generally cost more than an arranged overdraft but less than a credit card.

If you own property, you may be able to get a cheaper personal loan if you don't mind offering up your home as security.

With a personal loan the amount you borrow is paid back with regular monthly payments over a number of years. For smaller items, like televisions and video recorders, loans are usually paid back over three years. If you are borrowing money to buy a car or for improving your home, the loan is usually repaid over five years. There are almost as many ways to borrow money as to skin a cat. Chapter 6, *Borrowing Money*, shows you how to find the best way to borrow.

All the big banks now lend money for buying a house. The banks and the building societies don't use the same method for working out the repayments which makes it difficult to compare rates of interest. See Chapter 9, *Buying a Home*.

Several of the big banks offer a new variant on the old-fashioned budget account. These are designed to help you budget for your regular bills. You save a regular monthly amount out of which you pay your bills, and if there is ever a shortfall, the bank gives you a temporary overdraft.

With the new-style accounts you still pay in a regular amount each month. But there is a new twist, an automatic credit limit. The account gives you the right to borrow up to 30 times your monthly payment. For example, if you pay in £50 a month, you can borrow up to £1,500.

It's a good idea, but the service isn't cheap. The rate of interest you earn when the account is in credit is less than with a building society, and you are charged each time you write a cheque. The cost of borrowing is less than with a bank credit card, but higher than an arranged overdraft. There are better ways of budgeting (see Chapter 4, *Budgeting*) and better ways to borrow.

## The electronic age

With all this plastic money, is the cheque book about to become extinct? Barclays took the first step when they introduced the first plastic *debit card* – Barclays Connect – and Lloyds Bank plan to introduce one during the summer of 1988. With a debit card, instead of writing a cheque in a shop, you hand over your card, and it transfers money out of your account and into the shop's account.

You can also buy railway tickets and petrol by feeding your Barclaycard into a machine.

You may soon be able to carry a joint card which allows you to choose whether you use your current account or your credit card account.

The banks say it is coming but will be a long time in arriving. The investment, in new equipment in stores and new computer systems, runs into billions of pounds.

But when you think how quickly the big food stores introduced bar codes and laser scanning at the checkout, the death of the cheque book may be closer than you think.

## Financial fraud

In an era of rising street crime, who picks up the tab if someone fraudulently uses your cheque book, building society passbook, or your plastic cards go missing?

The greatest danger is when you don't notice something is missing. Even in these circumstances the banks don't make you foot the bill if someone uses your cheque book and manages to get money out of your bank account. Cheque book fraud is generally easy to demonstrate, the evidence is there on the cheque which the bank keeps. However, you may have more difficulty proving that someone used your cash dispenser card without your permission, so make sure you always know where it is and if you can, keep a mental note of your PIN number.

If your credit card is used before you let the credit card company know it is missing, they may ask you to bear some of the loss – usually the first £50.

The building societies take a much tougher line. You are responsible for your passbook. If it goes missing and someone uses it fraudulently, you are responsible for the loss, not the building society. But it is quite difficult to get money out of a building society account. Most passbooks contain your signature which can only be read with an ultra violet light. The cashier checks this against the signature on the withdrawal slip.

You can now register your credit cards and insure them against any loss. If you lose your credit cards all you do is tell the registry and they inform the credit card companies. However, unless you carry a lot of credit cards, the cost isn't justified.

# 4

# BUDGETING

Our grandmothers relied on jam jars on the mantelpiece. With weekly amounts put aside for gas, clothes, coal, electricity, holidays and Christmas, the jam jar was the essential tool of family budgeting.

Bank accounts and monthly pay cheques put the jam jar out of business. Now the headaches arise because your need for money doesn't necessarily coincide with the arrival of your monthly pay cheque. You need it when the bills come in, and you need it in big dollops at holiday time and Christmas.

Then there is the age of the plastic card adding a new dimension and further complicating all our best efforts to balance our books.

Do you approach the end of the month with trepidation? Do you wait for that letter from the bank manager? Do you curse your credit cards each time you see how much interest you are clocking up? Are you forever being tempted by in-store credit cards which commit you to heavy monthly payments in exchange for an expensive line in credit?

If this is you, remember the banks and the finance houses need mugs like you – that's how they earn their money. Decide to turn the tables on them. Get your bank account and plastic cards to serve you, not enslave you.

### Monitor your spending

The first step on the road to financial sanity is often the most difficult. Start with last year. Take a large sheet of paper, your payslips, cheque stubs, bank and credit card statements and your bills. If you don't keep them, start now.

On one side note your income, on the other what you spent it on, dividing your expenditure into essential and non-essential items. See in particular how much you wasted paying bank charges, and interest.

On page 53 there is a budget planner. Use it or adapt it to your own circumstances.

If you aren't reaching for the tranquillisers by now, you will have a good idea of how much of each month's pay cheque ought to be earmarked for essential bills. For some of us that knowledge is all we need to keep us on the straight and narrow and out of debt. Others need to reinvent the jam jar on the mantelpiece.

Aim to pay no bank charges and no interest to the credit card companies. To get free banking all you need do is keep your account in the black. That way the banks won't charge you each time you write a cheque, pay a standing order or direct debit.

## Control your credit cards

Next take a critical look at the bits of plastic in your handbag or wallet. The different credit cards and how they work are explained in Chapter 6, *Borrowing Money*. Be clear on which you have.

Make your credit cards work for you. If you can, repay your credit card debts out of savings – you are likely to be paying a much higher rate of interest on your borrowings than you are earning on your savings.

Give up any revolving store credit cards. You will invariably end up out of pocket – only a handful pay you interest while you are in credit. And it's an expensive way to borrow money.

Throw away, too, any charge cards with an annual service charge. If you need the card in your job for buying expensive items such as airline tickets, get your employer to pay the annual fee.

Keep your Access and Visa cards. But be firm – use them like a charge card and clear the account each month. That way you get up to 56 days' free credit, and it's you not the bank who has the last laugh.

## Save for bills

If you are one of those people who regrets the passing of the jam jar, try setting aside a monthly amount with that good old standby, a building society. There is no charge for opening an account, and these days you can find accounts which combine a reasonable rate of interest with some of the features you normally expect to find only with a cheque account, such as standing orders, cash cards, and in some cases cheques as well.

These accounts don't offer the full cheque account service now on offer from the Abbey National and Nationwide, but they do offer a higher rate of interest which makes them definitely worth thinking about if you want a second bank account to help you budget for bills. In some cases, most notably, the Abbey National, Halifax and Woolwich, you can pay your bills through a cash dispenser.

Avoid the clearing banks' own budget accounts. With these you transfer a regular monthly amount from your current account. You use the account for paying bills, and the bank covers any temporary shortfall with an overdraft. Budget accounts have gone out of fashion and only a couple of the big banks now offer them. And they are expensive, with a high minimum yearly fee.

The banks' own revolving credit schemes are a better bet, so long as you can keep them in credit, when they pay you interest. They work in much the same way as in-store credit cards, except you can usually borrow up to 30 times your monthly payment.

But beware – the banks charge you each time you make a withdrawal, and you need to keep a fairly high average balance or write relatively few cheques, before the banks start paying you money rather than the other way round.

Avoid *savings stamps*. You can buy television licence, road tax and telephone savings stamps at the post office, and in some areas you can get stamps for home helps and water rates as well. You stick them on to a special card and put them towards the cost of your next bill. Most gas and electricity boards sell similar savings stamps through their showrooms.

You don't earn interest when you buy savings stamps, so if you need to put a regular amount to one side to pay for your bills, you are much better putting it where you will earn interest.

## Spreading costs

The alternative is to arrange a budget account with British Telecom, gas and electricity boards. Instead of paying your bills quarterly, you spread them over 12 equal monthly payments with a standing order from your bank.

The electricity and gas boards look at how much gas and electricity you used last year. They then work out how much your bills are likely to come to this year and divide the figure into 12 equal monthly instalments. At the end of the year your account is adjusted, up or down, depending on the actual size of your bills.

Quarterly gas and electricity bills effectively give you up to three months' free credit because you use the gas and electricity before you pay for it. With monthly budget accounts you reduce that free credit to just a month.

However, your bills may fluctuate during the year. For example, with gas central heating, your two winter gas bills will be much higher than those in the summer. If this happens to you, think about taking out a budget account at the beginning of the winter. This way you spread the heavy cost of those winter quarters over the whole year.

*Rates* are such a major item of household expenditure that you now have the right to pay your rates bill by regular instalments.

Most local authorities send out their rates bills with a demand for half the money in April and the other half in October. If you want to spread the payments over a longer period you can. The legislation which gave ratepayers the right to pay rates by instalments is not clear, but most local authorities let you pay in 10 equal monthly instalments. They are not allowed to charge you any extra for this service, so the advantage is all yours and you should take it.

You can also spread the cost of car, buildings and house contents insurance over 12 monthly instalments paid either by standing order or direct debit. Even if the insurance company charges you extra for paying monthly, you may be better off.

Look at all your yearly bills which you pay as a lump sum in advance. With these bills you lose the use of that money for the rest of the year, when it could be sitting in a savings account earning money. Ask if you can pay by instalments.

## Budget planner

INCOME

£

After tax income from employment:
  PAYE earnings
  Freelance and self-employed earnings

After tax income from savings and investments

Any other income – such as Child Benefit or
other State benefits, alimony or child
maintenance payments, income from investment
property                                   _____

TOTAL INCOME                       _____

EXPENDITURE

*Essentials*                                                           £
   Food
   Mortgage or rent
   Rates and water rates
   Electricity
   Gas
   Other fuels
   Telephone
   National Insurance contributions
   Pension contributions
   House maintenance
   Buildings and house contents insurance
   Travelling to work
   Child care
   Clothes

Total essential expenditure

*Non-essentials* £
   Holidays
   Drink and cigarettes
   Entertaining and meals out
   Presents
   Car purchase
   Car maintenance
   Car insurance and road tax
   Petrol
   Travel not already allowed for
   School fees
   Home improvements
   Housekeeping
   Professional fees
   Trade union dues or subscriptions to professional bodies
   Life insurance
   Regular savings plans
   Personal Equity Plans
   Other investments acquired
   Newspapers, books and periodicals
   TV rental and/or licence
   Hobbies
   Loan repayments
   Bank and credit card interest
   Children's pocket money
   Your own pocket money

Total non-essential expenditure

TOTAL EXPENDITURE

EXCESS (OR OTHERWISE) OF INCOME OVER EXPENDITURE

# 5

# SAVING

If you find it difficult to save money, you are not alone. Most of us live to the limit of our pay packets and beyond, terrified that those end-of-month cheques will reach our bank account before our salary goes in.

If you are living on a financial knife edge can you afford to save? Does it matter? And what do we mean by saving, anyway?

Think of saving as money you put by today to buy things which you want tomorrow. When you are young it's impossible to get excited about saving money when you know you won't see it again for 20 years.

But if you think of saving as a way of putting money by for a good holiday, or for that motorbike, the notion is not nearly so peculiar or so painful.

Look at your budget planner again (Chapter 4, *Budgeting*); is there anything you could trim? Aim to save between 10 and 15 per cent of your take-home pay. Once into a good savings routine, the habit will stay with you for life. You may start saving for the short-term, but you may soon find the long-term looking after itself.

When you start saving, keep it simple. Choose between National Savings, building societies, and the banks. If you pay basic-rate tax, you should shop around for the best rate of interest. If you don't pay tax, your best deal is usually a National Savings Investment Account or Income Bonds.

National Savings, the buildings societies and the banks all now offer a bewildering range of different savings plans.

To help you choose, the schemes have been divided into two

SAVING

# MORTGAGES

A flexible range of Mortgages
- REPAYMENT
- ENDOWMENT
- PENSION PLAN

Tailored to your needs.

Come in and talk to us at any of our branches.

*That's what we can do for you!*

**Bank of Ireland**

ASK NOW FOR DETAILS

Written quotations on request.

MANAGING YOUR MONEY

## PORT OUT, STARBOARD HOME...

If you share our commitment to the highest standards of integrity and excellence, perhaps you should talk to us about specialist financial advice.

**By choosing to invest your money with Deacon Hoare & Company Limited, you will not only receive V.I.P. financial advice and expertise to safeguard your investments, you may, as a bonus, use the exclusive, personal services of our associate travel company to advantage when contemplating the use of the benefits of your investment. An ocean cruise for example...**

Deacon Hoare offer term deposit, current account, currency, travel insurance and loan facilities. Private banking services available to selected clients.

### DEACON HOARE

Equity & Law House, 28, Baldwin Street,
BRISTOL BS1 1NG. Tel: (0272) 277478

---

## ASHTON ASSOCIATES

(FIMBRA MEMBER)

### FINANCIAL CONSULTANTS

**49/50 Hawley Square, Margate.
Telephone: (0843) 299058**

### 'INDEPENDENT FINANCIAL ADVISERS'

Mortgages, Insurance, Savings Plans,
Investments, Venture Capital,
Procurement Finance.

Licensed by the Department of Fair Trading
**PERSONAL AND CONFIDENTIAL SERVICE**

SAVING

# SPECIAL
# DEPOSIT ACCOUNTS

## Competitive Fixed Rates for periods up to 364 days

Apply now for our rate list

### INDUSTRIAL FUNDING TRUST LTD
70/74 CITY ROAD LONDON EC1Y 2BJ
TEL 01-253 7272
(Authorised Institution under the Banking Act 1987)

### BRIAN FOSTER & ASSOCIATES
(Member of F.I.M.B.R.A.)

**OFFER TOTALLY INDEPENDENT ADVICE ON ALL YOUR FINANCIAL PLANNING REQUIREMENTS**

- RETIREMENT PLANNING
- PORTFOLIO MANAGEMENT
- SCHOOL FEE PLANNING
- TAXATION SPECIALISATION
- MORTGAGES ● GUARANTEED INCOME

(FIMBRA MEMBER)

*For all your Financial Requirements*
TELEPHONE: 021-377 7922   021-778 4231   021-422 0101   0543-414241
OR WRITE

Please send me details of _____
Name _____
Address _____
_____
_____
Tel No _____

BRIAN FOSTER &
ASSOCIATES
FREEPOST
B72 1BR

MANAGING YOUR MONEY

| Branch | | | E/D B/S | Roll Number 2/ 18300 398 − 3 | | |
|---|---|---|---|---|---|---|
| Name and Address | | | | Paid-up Shares | | |
| date | cashier | office | details | withdrawals | receipts | balance |
| 1 | | | | | | |
| 2 | | | | | | |
| 3 | | | | | | |
| 4 | | | | | | |
| 5 | | | | | | |
| 6 | | | | | | |
| 7 | | | | | | |
| 8 | | | | | | |
| 9 | | | | | | |
| 10 | | | | | | |
| 11 | | | | | | |
| 12 | | | | | | |
| 13 | | | | | | |

CANCELLED

sections: those which are suitable if you want to save a regular amount each month, and those which are suitable if you have a lump sum to invest. The division is somewhat arbitrary, with some schemes suitable for both regular saving and lump sum investment. However, novice savers should begin their search among the regular savings plans.

Remember, banks and building societies pay you interest with basic-rate tax already taken off. If you don't pay tax you can't claim it back. If you pay higher-rate tax there is extra tax to pay.

With National Savings your interest is paid gross with no tax deducted. This often gives the best rate of interest if you don't pay tax. You must declare any taxable interest from National Savings accounts and Income and Deposit Bonds to the Inland Revenue. National Savings Save As You Earn, Savings Certificates, Yearly Plans, and winnings on Premium Bonds are all tax free and don't need to be declared. If you pay tax, they will send you a tax bill, or make an adjustment to your Notice of Coding and collect the interest through your pay packet. See Chapter 2, *The Inland Revenue*.

The rate of return on most savings plans is not fixed and goes up and down with any change in interest rates. There are exceptions. For example, the interest rate on the National Savings Certificates and Yearly Plans is fixed when you take out the plan. It is worth going for this kind of savings plan when interest rates are high, because you continue to get a good rate of interest when other interest rates fall.

## Regular savings plans

NATIONAL SAVINGS BANK

*Ordinary account*
You can open an account with just £1 at any post office. You can put in and take out money as and when you want. The interest rate is not high, but the first £70 of interest is tax free, which can make it good value for certain higher-rate taxpayers. If you can keep your balance above £500 for the whole of 1988, the interest rate is 5 per cent. Below that it falls to 2.5 per cent.

*Yearly Plan*
A regular savings plan which you take out for at least a year. You agree to pay at least £20 a month, and there is a maximum of £200 a month. At the end of the year you can cash the plan with interest or continue it and earn a higher rate of interest for another four

MANAGING YOUR MONEY

## WILMOT DOLLAR ASSOCIATES

### Financial & Investment Consultants

#### WE SPECIALIZE IN:—

- Tax efficient investment ● Portfolio planning
- Inheritance Tax planning
- School fees provision ● Planning for expatriates
- Pension provision ● Domestic & Commercial Mortgages
- Commercial Finance

**FOR FREE ADVICE PLEASE CONTACT:—**

Brian J. W. Dollar
Principal

18 Eversley Road
Bexhill-on-sea
East Sussex TN40 IHE

FIMBRA MEMBER

Tel: (0424) 210447
Fax: (0424) 730668
Telex: 95369 NORMEC G

---

## *FLEMING ASSOCIATES*
43 Brunswick Hill, Macclesfield SK10 1ET
CREDIT CONSUMER LICENCE No. 218717

### LIZ FLEMING
ALIA (DIP)

ON
**0625 611791**

LIFE ASSURANCE, MORTGAGES & RE-MORTGAGES
HOUSEHOLD AND FINANCIAL PLANNING
PENSIONS AND BUSINESS SERVICES

For personal and friendly service in the
privacy of your own home or office, contact
your local Independant Financial Advisor.

FIMBRA MEMBER

years. The rate of interest is fixed at the beginning of the term. The interest is not taxable and if you keep the plan going for five years the interest rate is 7 per cent.

*4th Index-Linked Certificates*
Nicknamed granny bonds, they can be bought in units of £10. The value of the bonds is linked to the retail price index. You must hold the bonds for a year before you get the value of the indexation. There is an additional bonus on top of inflation of 3 per cent after the first year rising to 6 per cent after five years. Granny bonds were a good deal when inflation raged. Now their value is boosted with special bonuses to keep them competitive with other savings plans. The interest is tax free.

*Investment Account*
You can open an Investment Account at any post office with £5. If you want to take money out you must give one month's notice in writing to the NSB Headquarters in Glasgow. Get the repayment form and a prepaid envelope at the post office. The interest is taxable and the rate is 8.5 per cent.

BUILDING SOCIETIES

*Ordinary or deposit accounts*
These are sometimes known as ordinary shares, or paid-up share accounts. This is the simplest type of building society account. You can open one with just £1, and put money in and take it out as and when you please. Many people now use these accounts instead of a bank account, although you won't get a cheque book. Don't keep large amounts in a building society ordinary account. The interest rate is low, when compared with other building society accounts. Building societies vary in the amount of interest they pay, but the interest rate on ordinary accounts is around 4 per cent.

*Regular monthly savings accounts*
These are sometimes known as subscription or bonus share accounts. You agree to pay a regular amount of money each month, in return for a slightly higher rate of interest than that available on the ordinary share account. The minimum is usually quite small. You can arrange to do this with a standing order from your bank account. They are a good idea if you want a scheme which discourages early withdrawal. With this account you only get all your money back when you close the account, although most societies allow you to dip

MANAGING YOUR MONEY

## The GLA Group

# 'MANAGING YOUR MONEY' MUST SUIT YOU!

## Chris Leach & Associates Ltd

**Independent Personal and Corporate Financial Advisers**

**CLA House, 11 Windsor Place, Cardiff CF1 1YU**

(FIMBRA MEMBER)

*"You are an individual, and therefore financial plans must be 'tailor made' to suit your own situation"*
— details available on request —

(or perhaps you would just like to talk informally with one of us)

---

Please send me FREE details of how Managing My Money can be 'tailor made' for me

Name ..................................................................................................

Address ..............................................................................................

............................................................................................................

Send to: C.L.A. FREEPOST, 11 Windsor Place, Cardiff CF1 1YU
or Tel: (0222) 341531/2 or 395042/6.   Fax: (0222) 388155

---

## HANNAM HATTON ASSOCIATES
### INDEPENDENT FINANCIAL ADVISERS

**215 MARSH ROAD · PINNER · MIDDLESEX HA5 5NE**
Tel: 01-868 1416 · Fax: 01-429 3470

Our personal service specialises in advising individuals and companies on all aspects of Pensions, Life Assurance, Mortgages and Investment in Unit Trusts, Insurance Bonds and Share Dealing.

(FIMBRA MEMBER)

Partners:
J. E. C. Hannam
B. R. Hatton, M.A.(Cantab)

Registered Insurance Broker

into the account between one and three times a year without closing the account, and some pay a bonus if you go a whole year without making a withdrawal. Interest rate around 5 per cent.

*Save As You Earn (SAYE) 2nd Issue*
You agree to pay between £1 and £20 a month for five years. At the end of five years you get a bonus of 14 months' payments tax free. Keep the money in for a further two years and your bonus is doubled. On the face of it this looks like a good deal. The rate of interest over five years is 8.3 per cent, rising to 8.6 per cent if you keep it in for seven years.

*Gold account*
Each building society has its own name for this type of account. So look out for names like Five Star, Prime, Sovereign and Extra-Ordinary. They pay a higher rate of interest than ordinary accounts, but you need a higher minimum investment, commonly between £250 and £1,000. Once you have saved enough money in your ordinary account, trade up to a Gold account. You can get your money out of a Gold account whenever you like, without penalty. The interest rate often increases the more you have invested. The rate of interest varies between 5.75 and 7.5 per cent.

THE BANKS

*Deposit account*
Sometimes referred to as seven-day deposit account; offered by all banks. You can open an account with just £1. You must give seven days' notice that you want to withdraw money. You can get money out on demand but you lose seven days' interest on the sum withdrawn. The interest rate is 2.5 to 3 per cent.

*Deposit account with a cash card*
Offered by most of the big banks. You can open an account with just £1 and you don't need to hold a current account with the bank. You can withdraw money on demand through a cash dispenser, normally without penalty. You may lose seven days' interest with other withdrawals. The rate of interest is similar to a deposit account.

*Regular monthly savings account*
Not offered by all banks. The minimum investment is usually £10 a month for at least a year. The rate of interest is generally above the seven-day deposit rate. Some plans permit several partial withdraw-

als each year. Others allow no withdrawals in first or second years without loss of interest. Interest rates are between 3.5 and 4 per cent.

*Mortgage savings account*
Not offered by all banks, and the schemes vary, but similar to a regular monthly savings account. You agree to pay a regular amount into the account each month. In return you are guaranteed a mortgage, which can be useful in times of mortgage shortages. You need to have your current account with the bank. Several partial withdrawals are normally allowed each year without suffering loss of interest. Rates of interest are similar to regular savings accounts.

All these savings schemes are suitable if you want to save a regular amount each month. You can narrow your choice still further by asking yourself some simple questions.

- Will I need the money in the next six months or so?
  If so, choose an account with easy access, or a savings scheme which doesn't reduce your interest rate if you make a partial withdrawal.
- Am I disciplined enough to put aside a regular amount of money each month?
  If the answer is no, go for the type of savings plan where you commit yourself to save a regular amount each month, and pay it by standing order.
- Am I saving for a deposit on a house?
  If this is the case, don't necessarily go for the highest rate of interest. Instead, save with the bank or building society where you hope to get your mortgage. Not all building societies have the same lending policies. If you think you might want to buy a run-down house, or a converted flat, or anything slightly out of the ordinary, make sure the bank or building society is willing to lend on this type of property.

Aim to have an emergency fund which you can get your hands on quickly. Think in terms of a figure between two and three times your gross monthly salary. You never know when you might need it. It could be a patch of dry rot in your house, or your car blowing up on the motorway, or you may need to take unpaid leave from your job to nurse a sick parent for a month or two.

## Lump sum investment

Now you have got into the swing of saving regularly, where is the best place to put big sums of money? It could be money left you by a kind old aunt, a winning Premium Bond or a savings plan reaching maturity.

Once again you must hunt out the best rate of interest. Many of the accounts which can be used for regular savings can also be used for investing lump sums. These are:

National Savings Investment Account
National Savings Ordinary Account
National Savings 2nd Index-Linked Certificates
Premium Bonds
Building society share account
Building society gold account
Bank deposit account
Bank cash card deposit account

But there are others too.

NATIONAL SAVINGS

*Deposit Bond*
You can invest a minimum of £100. To earn the full rate of interest the money must remain invested for at least a year. The interest rate is halved if the bond is cashed in the first year. You must give three months' notice when you want your money back. The interest rate is 9 per cent and it's taxable.

*Income Bond*
The interest is paid as a monthly income. The minimum investment is £2,000. As with deposit bonds the money must remain invested for at least a year otherwise the interest rate is halved. You must also give three months' notice when you want your money back. The interest rate is also 9 per cent and it's taxable.

*National Savings Certificates 33rd Issue*
Issued in units of £25. The most you can hold is £1,000, or £5,000 if you are reinvesting a maturing certificate. The rate of interest increases the longer you hold the certificates, up to a maximum of five years. There is no interest until the end of the first year. Withdrawal takes about two weeks. The interest is tax free which makes it suitable for higher-rate taxpayers. The rate of interest is 7 per cent if you hold them for the full five years.

*Premium Bonds*
A lottery: the minimum holding is £10, the maximum £10,000. The

DOES YOUR PORTFOLIO NEED A TONIC?
ARE YOU RUNNING SHY OF TODAY'S
VOLATILE MARKET CONDITIONS?
AS INDEPENDENT INTERNATIONAL
FINANCIAL ADVISORS WE ARE IN
AN IDEAL POSITION TO GIVE YOU AN UNBIASED
OPINION ON YOUR PORTFOLIO.
SECURITY, FLEXIBILITY AND CONSTANT
MONITORING ARE THE CORNERSTONE OF OUR
INVESTMENT POLICY.

IF THAT SUITS YOU — CONTACT US TODAY

*ASHTON ASSOCIATES (KENT)*

4a Lewes Road, Bromley Kent BR1 2RW
01-460 0102

---

# Pensions advice that's not just impartial. It's free.

## Connaught Fine Ltd

INDEPENDENT    SALARIED    FINANCIAL    ADVISERS

72 Chatham Road
London SW11 6HG                    Tel: 01-924 3100

pay out is 6.5 per cent of the money invested.

BUILDING SOCIETIES

*Monthly income account*
Some building societies offer a monthly income as a separate account, others as a facility available with one of their other accounts. The minimum investment is between £500 and £1,000. You normally have to give one month's notice to get your money back.

*Notice account*
Often called Extra Interest or Special account. The notice period is anything from one to six months. The minimum investment is usually around £500. When you want your money back you must give the building society the agreed amount of notice, so if you agree to give six months' notice, you get your money back six months after asking for it. If you do need the money in a hurry you sacrifice the interest corresponding to the notice period. The interest rate sometimes increases the more money you invest. The interest rate is between 6.75 and 8 per cent.

THE BANKS

*High interest cheque account*
Offered by some banks; a minimum of at least £1,000 is needed to open one of these accounts. The rate of interest is between 2.5 and 6 per cent and normally increases the more you have invested.

*High interest deposit account*
Like a seven-day deposit account, but the minimum investment is usually at least £1,000. The interest rate is between 5 and 6 per cent and increases the more you have invested. You must give seven days' notice of any withdrawal. With instant withdrawals you lose seven days' interest.

*Notice account*
Also called Investment Account, Extra Interest or Monthly Income. Minimum investment between £1,000 and £5,000. Available with notice periods of between three weeks and six months. If you withdraw early you lose the interest you would have earned in the notice period. Rates of interest similar to high interest deposit accounts.

MANAGING YOUR MONEY

# MONEY CONCEPTS

*MONEY MANAGEMENT COULD
SERIOUSLY IMPROVE YOUR WEALTH*

**MONEY CONCEPTS**
INTERNATIONAL FINANCIAL PLANNING NETWORK

For details contact:-
**MONEY CONCEPTS INTERNATIONAL LTD**
**FREEPOST**
**LONDON E1 9RB**
**01-480 7304**

*Term account*
The rate of interest is normally fixed for the entire period. You tie up your money for a fixed period – it could be anything from one month to two years – in return for a higher rate of interest. You get your money back at the end of the term. Some banks give you the money back early if you have a good excuse, but they will reduce the interest rate, usually to the level of a seven-day deposit account. Rates of interest are similar to high interest deposit accounts.

FINANCE HOUSES
Finance houses are mini-banks but without the branch network of the big clearing banks. You see their advertisements in the newspapers offering deposit accounts similar to those from the clearing banks, but often with slightly higher rates of interest. Any company which takes deposits from the public must be licensed by the Bank of England, and there is a compensation scheme if anything should go wrong. See page 80.

INSURANCE COMPANIES

*Income and growth bonds*
With these you agree to invest money with an insurance company for a fixed period of time, in return for a rate of interest which is fixed at the outset. The minimum investment can be anything between £500 and £2,500 and the term varies from two to 10 years. Income and growth bonds offer good value if you take them out when interest rates are high. But avoid tying up your money for more than five years, just in case interest rates go up by more than you expected. Interest rates are between 6 and 7 per cent.

All these savings plans have one thing in common: when you ask for your money back, you get it all back. You are not putting your savings at risk.

## Becoming an investor

Once you have mastered the ins and outs of National Savings, the building societies and banks, you may feel you now deserve to have a little fun with your money. You are now ready to think about investing in company shares or government stocks.

These are a much riskier form of investment, because there is no guarantee that you will get all your money back when you need it.

## MANAGING YOUR MONEY

---

**(FIMBRA MEMBER)**

# CHILDS & COMPANY  ⓙ

### THE BUILDING SOCIETY BROKER

### INDEPENDENT FINANCIAL ADVISERS

WITH EIGHT LOCAL OFFICES, CHILDS & CO ARE DEVON'S LARGEST INDEPENDENT FINANCIAL ADVISERS. WE GIVE FREE AND IMPARTIAL ADVICE ON ALL MONEY MATTERS, FROM BUILDING SOCIETY INVESTMENTS AND MORTGAGES TO STOCKS AND SHARES, UNIT TRUSTS, INVESTMENT BONDS, LIFE ASSURANCE, PENSIONS AND ANNUITIES.

**For a free review of your investments, Call in or phone our offices at**

| Exeter | Exmouth | Crediton | Sidmouth |
|---|---|---|---|
| 0392-211800 | 0395-276740 | 03632-5717 | 03955-78211 |
| **Seaton** | **Ottery St. Mary** | **Brixham** | **Honiton** |
| 0297-20821 | 040481-5551 | 08045-55818 | 0404-2188 |

---

### COMPANY SHARES

The price of shares of a company quoted on the Stock Exchange goes up and down. When you invest in them, if they go up you stand to make money, but if they go down you will be out of pocket.

The price of company shares is affected by all sorts of factors: whether the company is doing well; whether the stock market as a whole is thriving.

A lot of people got their first taste of buying company shares when they subscribed for shares in companies such as British Telecom, Trustee Savings Bank, British Airways and British Gas, when they were first offered for sale.

Buying shares in new issues is easy; all you do is fill in the coupon in the newspaper and cross your fingers that you strike lucky in the ensuing lottery. It's when you want to sell them, or buy other shares, that the problems begin.

You could try your bank. All the banks have a share dealing service, but it may cost you more than going directly to a stockbroker.

You can find a stockbroker by writing to The International Stock Exchange, London EC2N 1HP, telephone 01-588 2355, who produce a useful booklet 'An Introduction to the Stock Market'. It costs £1.00

**BRASS CASTLE CONSULTANTS LTD**
Insurance, Finance and Investment Consultants.
Licensed Credit Brokers.

Brass Castle Hill, 80 Market Street, Pocklington
York YO4 2AB
Tel: (0759) 303713

(make cheques payable to The International Stock Exchange) and it has a list of brokers who are willing to take on new private clients.

Stockbrokers make their living by charging their clients a commission when they buy and sell shares. If all you need is a share dealing service and you don't want any help or advice, shop around for the stockbroker with the cheapest commission. It's worth knowing that out-of-town stockbrokers often work out cheaper than London brokers.

GOVERNMENT STOCKS

When you buy government stocks, often referred to as gilts, you are effectively lending money to the government. The price of government stocks fluctuates with interest rates. When interest rates fall, the price of government stocks tends to rise. The reverse is true when interest rates rise: the price of the stock tends to fall.

You can also buy government stocks through your bank or stockbroker. But there is another route, which is cheaper if you don't want to invest a vast sum. You can buy government stocks through the National Savings Stock Register. You can get a form and list of government stocks on the register from the post office. Ask for leaflet DNS 708/85/01 and form GS1 and prepaid envelope GS3M when you are buying and form GS3 when you are selling.

MANAGING YOUR MONEY

---

## THE · YORKSHIRE · UNIT · TRUST
## MANAGERS · LIMITED

| UTA MEMBER | | LAUTRO MEMBER | IMRO MEMBER |

**The Yorkshire Central Unit Trust**
Invests 75% of its funds in Yorkshire quoted companies. Since launch in January 1986 unit price has increased by over 77%. Offer to bid (22nd June 1988). Approximately £9m invested.

**The Yorkshire Central Income Trust**
Invests in UK Equities/Convertibles.
Above average income.
Possibility of capital growth.

Minimum investment in both funds £500
NEW Monthly Savings Plan available for both trusts — Minimum £25 per month

**Telephone 0484 602250 for more information and an application form**

Unit Trust investment should be regarded as medium term.
The price of units may go down as well as up
Prices quoted daily in *The Financial Times, Daily Telegraph* and *Yorkshire Post*

*A MEMBER OF THE BWD SECURITIES PLC GROUP*

Registered Office: Woodsome House, Woodsome Park, Fenay Bridge, Huddersfield HD8 0JG
Tel: (0484) 602250
VAT Reg. No. 427 3580 47. Registered in England 1938417.

---

# HARALD OSTHOFF & ASSOCIATES
# COMPANY LIMITED

Registered with:
The Association of Futures Brokers & Dealers Ltd

**We specialise in advising private clients on all aspects of the Option Markets for all the commodities and financial markets.**

## MINIMUM ACCOUNT £2,000

Whether you are interested in Puts or Calls why not call us to put you in the picture?

Harald Osthoff & Associates Co Ltd
Bishops House
The Market Place           Telephone: 0753 887243 887135
Chalfont St Peter          Fax: 0753 889078
Bucks SL9 9HE              Telex: 0846212

When you buy government stocks through the National Savings Stock Register the interest is paid gross without any deduction for tax, which is useful for people who pay no tax. When you buy government stocks through your bank or stockbroker the interest is paid net after a deduction is made for basic-rate tax.

UNIT TRUSTS

If you don't know which share to buy but like the idea of investing in company shares, you could try putting your money in a unit trust, or several unit trusts.

Unit trusts invest in a spread of company shares. The trust is then divided up into equal units. When you invest in a unit trust you buy the number of units which corresponds with the amount of money you want to invest. The price of the units moves up and down depending on the stock market value of all its investments. If the fund is successful it will outperform the stock market as a whole. And just like shares, you make money when the price of your units goes up, and lose money when the price goes down.

The minimum investment in unit trusts is anywhere between £100 and £5,000, depending on the trust.

Choosing a unit trust is a daunting task. There are now over 1100 to go for. It's a good idea to consult one of the specialist magazines, such as *Money Management* or *Planned Savings*. If your local reference library doesn't keep them, you will find their addresses in Appendix 1.

Many unit trust groups also operate regular savings schemes. With these you undertake to invest a certain amount each month. The minimum in some cases is as low as £10 a month. You can continue or stop the plan whenever you like. Unit trust savings plans are not a good place to put your money if you want to make frequent withdrawals.

The trick is to cash in your plan when the stock market is riding high. If you can keep the plan going for at least seven years you are likely to do better than saving the same amount regularly with National Savings, a bank or a building society.

INSURANCE BONDS

Until recently unit trusts were not permitted to invest in property. Insurance companies were, which led to the development of insurance bonds. The first insurance bonds invested in property. Others followed investing in company shares, fixed interest investments, and managed funds which invest in a little of everything.

Property bonds are still the principal way of investing in commercial property. The fund managers behind a managed bond can switch funds between property, shares and fixed interest stocks to take advantage of changing market sentiment. If they get it right, and it always is a big if, the fund will do well. None of the other funds offer any particular advantage.

GOLD

Gold is another popular long-term investment. British citizens are prevented by law from owning gold bullion. The nearest you get to owning gold bullion is when you buy gold coins. The South African Krugerrand, the Canadian Maple, and the home-grown Sovereign and Britannia all closely reflect the price of gold on the world's bullion market, as do the less popular new-style US Eagle and the Australian Nugget.

You can buy gold coins through your bank, or through a coin dealer such as Spink & Son. Gold coins are normally subject to value added tax, so your coin must rise in value by at least 15 per cent before you start showing a profit.

### Investment information

Knowing what's what in the world of savings and investment is the

---

# CITY FINANCE

### MORTGAGE AND INVESTMENT CONSULTANTS

*offer*

#### FREE HOME ADVISORY SERVICE

★ 100% Building society mortgages ★
★ Remortgages to raise capital
8¼% available ★
★ Commercial loans ★
★ Investment and Insurance ★
★ Personal loans ★
★ Council house purchases ★
★ Expatriates' mortgages available ★

#### PROBLEM CASES WELCOME

Mortgage arrears, county court judgements.
No accounts for self employed.

TEL: 0375-371808 (9am-5pm)
or 0277-210879, SAFFRON WALDEN 40678 (any time)

## R. S. & J. INSURANCE SERVICES (WALES) LIMITED

R. S. & J. House, 32 Blue Street, Carmarthen, Dyfed SA31 3LE.
Tel. 0267-230702 (7 lines)
Opening hours: 8.00 am to 6.00 pm MONDAY TO FRIDAY
8.00 am to 4.00 pm SATURDAY

### INDEPENDENT FINANCIAL ADVISORS AND GENERAL INSURANCE BROKERS

**LIFE INSURANCE:** Personal — Key Man — Partnership Protection
**PENSIONS:** Personal Plans — Group Schemes — A.V.C.'s.
**INVESTMENTS:** Unit Trusts — Investment Bonds — Building Society

**FULLY COMPUTERISED — PORTFOLIOS VALUED AND UPDATED DAILY.**

FIMBRA MEMBER

---

first step. You now need to know where to look for up-to-date information on rates of interest, and stock market prices.

*The Times, Financial Times, Daily Telegraph, Guardian* and *Independent* all run family money pages on a Saturday. Most weeks they run tables showing current interest rates. The *Sunday Times*, the *Observer*, and *Sunday Telegraph* do the same on Sunday. The *Daily Mail*, the *Express* and *Today* run their money pages on a Wednesday.

### How to complain

Bank managers have a talent for putting people's noses out of joint. So where do you go if you want to lodge a complaint against your bank manager? There is now a banking ombudsman who will arbitrate between you and your bank. Before the ombudsman takes on a case, he needs to know that you have taken your complaint right up to head office. And he won't get involved in questions of commercial judgement.

You are not bound by the ombudsman's decision. If you aren't satisfied you can pursue your case through the courts. The banks, on the other hand, agree to stand by his decision and he can make settlements of up to £50,000.

MANAGING YOUR MONEY

# Independent Financial Services

- ☐ Commercial Mortgages (High % Advance)
- ☐ Domestic Mortgages (up to 100%)
- ☐ Pension Planning
- ☐ *Unit Trust Investment & Management
- ☐ *Stocks & Shares/Special Situation/ Portfolio Review
- ☐ Portfolio Management Incl. PEP Schemes
- ☐ Life Assurance & Regular Savings

*These investments can go down as well as up

(FIMBRA MEMBER)

Whatever your Financial Needs we offer Independent Advice, backed up with Taxation Planning

Tick the item of interest and send this Advert, to one of the addresses below, or telephone us

**TFS TRUMARK FINANCIAL SERVICES LTD**

Field House, 8 Richmond Road, Exeter EX4 4JA
Telephone (0392) 412912

8 Angel Hill, Tiverton, Devon EX16 6PE
Telephone (0884) 253850 or 258980

Name
Address
Tel. No. (Day)
(Evening)

---

## MIDAS FINANCIAL SERVICES

23 St. Martin's Street, Wallingford, Oxon. OX10 0AL
Wallingford (0491) 36773

**WE ARE PLEASED TO OFFER ADVICE ON ALL FORMS OF PERSONAL FINANCIAL AND GENERAL AND GENERAL INSURANCE**

*Fast mortgage service for Private/Commercial Remortgages*

- Life Assurance and Pensions ● School fees planning
- Unit Trust Investments ● Retirement Income Plans

**COMPUTERISED QUOTATIONS FOR MORTGAGES LIFE AND MOTOR**

*Please telephone to discuss your needs*
*As a totally independent Intermediary you can count on a good deal from us*

(FIMBRA MEMBER)

**Table 5.1** Rates of interest for savers on 20 June 1988

| Savings account | No tax % | Tax at 25 per cent % | Tax at 40 per cent % |
|---|---|---|---|
| Building society ordinary accounts | 3.5 | 3.5 | 2.8 |
| Building society gold, and notice accounts | 5.0–7.5 | 5.0–7.5 | 4.0–6.0 |
| Building society regular savings plans | 4.5 | 4.5 | 3.6 |
| Building society Save As You Earn | 8.3 | 8.3 | 8.3 |
| Bank deposit accounts | 2.0 | 2.0 | 1.6 |
| Bank high interest deposit accounts | 4.6–5.8 | 4.6–5.8 | 3.7–4.6 |
| Bank term deposits | 5.1–7.3 | 5.1–7.3 | 4.1–5.8 |
| Guaranteed income bonds | 6.0–8.0 | 6.0–8.0 | 5.1–6.8 |
| National Savings Certificates 33rd issue held for five years | 7.0 | 7.0 | 7.0 |
| National Savings Ordinary Account  Below £500  £500 and above | 2.5  5.0 | 2.5[1]  5.0[1] | 2.5[1]  5.0[1] |
| National Savings Investment Account | 8.5 | 6.4 | 5.1 |
| National Savings Income Bond | 9.0 | 6.8 | 5.4 |
| National Savings Deposit Bond | 9.0 | 6.8 | 5.4 |
| National Savings Yearly Plan held for five years | 7.0 | 7.0 | 7.0 |

[1] First £70 of annual interest is tax free

The building societies and the insurance companies operate similar ombudsman schemes (addresses in Appendix 1). The insurance ombudsman doesn't cover all insurance companies, but most of the major companies do belong to the scheme.

What happens if something goes wrong, and through no fault of your own you lose your money?

With National Savings you should be as safe as houses. National Savings are guaranteed by the government.

Licensed banks and finance houses are regulated by the Bank of England and are covered by a compensation scheme which pays out 75 per cent of deposits up to £20,000.

As a building society saver you are slightly better protected. Building societies are regulated by the Building Societies Commission. If a building society goes bust there is a compensation scheme which pays out 90 per cent of deposits up to £20,000. Insurance companies which are authorised by the Department of Trade are covered by the Policyholders Protection Board. If a life insurance company goes bust the board pays 90 per cent of any outstanding claims. Policies still in force are transferred to other companies but benefits can be scaled down to 90 per cent of those payable under the old policy.

Don't put money with unauthorised overseas insurance companies. Some have gone bust and there is no compensation fund.

The International Stock Exchange has a long standing compensation scheme covering stock market investments which compensates investors if they have paid money to a stockbroker who then goes bust, owing money to clients.

A number of new compensation schemes, covering unit trusts, life insurance and investment managers, should be in force by 1988 under the banner of the Financial Services Act. The Act is administered by the Securities and Investments Board (SIB).

## FINANCIAL ADVICE — THE FACTS

**Q.** **WHERE CAN YOU GET:**
100% commission refunds ... personally tailored help on investments ... life assurance or pensions ... in-house income and capital tax advice ... a mortgage to suit you ... investment portfolio management ... truly INDEPENDENT advice?

**A.** **AT DONNE MILEHAM & HADDOCK**
(Financial Services Division) a large and progressive firm with 16 offices in Sussex.

*Contact us on Brighton (0273) 820803 or at the address below. We will send you information to help you make up your mind.*

**DM&H**

**DONNE MILEHAM & HADDOCK**
Frederick Place, Brighton
East Sussex BN1 1AT

Solicitors, regulated in the conduct of investment business by the Law Society

# THESIS
INDEPENDENT INVESTMENT MANAGERS AND INSURANCE ADVISERS

THESIS is a professionally managed and established firm with exceptional experience in caring for the investment needs of individuals in every walk of life, whether UK resident or non-resident and regardless of age.

THESIS has no commitment to any organization or product and its City-trained managers can therefore offer totally impartial advice on any size of fund with personal attention to the investor's circumstances and requirements.

A FIMBRA MEMBER

REGNUM HOUSE, 45 SOUTH STREET
CHICHESTER, WEST SUSSEX PO19 1DS
TELEPHONE
INVESTMENT (0243) 531234
INSURANCE (0243) 532834

# 6

# BORROWING MONEY

'Neither a borrower, nor a lender be.' It might sound like good advice, but is it really realistic?

There are even times when borrowing makes good financial sense, as it did during the 1970s when interest rates were often below the level of inflation. At times like these saving is a mug's game. Inflation erodes the value of your savings at a faster rate than the interest you can earn on it.

When inflation is high, it makes sound financial sense to borrow money because you pay the loan back with money which is fast losing its value.

Nowadays, with interest rates well above the level of inflation, the reverse is the case and the advantage belongs to the saver not the borrower. So before buying anything on tick, think carefully. Do you really need this thing you have set your heart on? And are you prepared to pay interest to have it now? Can it wait until you have saved the money to buy it outright?

Chapter 9, *Buying a Home*, guides you through the mortgage jungle as the banks and the building societies fight it out for your custom.

In this chapter you will find the best way to borrow money if you want to buy a car, a new three-piece suite, or a washing machine. Borrowing is never cheap, but some types of loan make a lot better sense than others.

## Comparing rates of interest

When you shop around for the cheapest way to borrow money,

## BORROWING MONEY

### R. H. Willis & Son

Personal Hire-Purchase or Credit Sale
facilities to individuals
(30 mile radius of Southampton)

Motor Cars, Touring Caravans, Boats etc may be purchased privately
We can advise on prices of Cars & Caravans
as we have the various price guides
Accident, Sickness & Redundancy insurance available
Telephone or personal call

*Members of the Consumer Credit Trade Association, and operating the Association's code of practice*

69 Morris Road, Southampton SO1 2BQ
Tel. Southampton (0703) 226823

Established 1965, in business since 1938

---

### Reduce the cost of your mortgage by 28% per month
### Mortgages and Remortgages

Capital Raising, Home Improvements, Credit Card and Loan Consolidation, New Car and Holiday Homes.

**RAISE CAPITAL FOR ANY PURPOSE**

| Example: | | COMMERCIAL LOANS — 10-25 years |
|---|---|---|
| £30,000 Mortgage from a typical building society/bank monthly repayments, approx. APR 10.4% | £227.05 | PERSONAL LOANS for home owners only. Self employed can obtain £10,000 without proof of income. Loans secured on property — New reduced rate |
| £30,000 Low start mortgage scheme monthly repayments approx. APR 10.6%. | £163.77 | 100% MORTGAGES at normal building society rates PENSION SPECIALISTS — Life Assurance discounts. |
| NET MONTHLY SAVING OF (subject to status) | £64.28 | TAX SAVING PENSION MORTGAGES |
| | | GUARANTEED 10% net monthly income on investment |

Call us now — Written details on request — NO FEES

**KEN WARD FINANCIAL SERVICES**
21 Cregagh Road, Belfast          Tel. 732711
5 Castle Street, Carrickfergus    Tel. 61020
The above offices are appointed representatives fo MGM Assurance

**KEN WARD & CO**
81 Belmont Road, Belfast          Tel. 651118

LAUTRO    IMRO

*The Office is an independent Brokerage and members of FIMBRA.*
*All offices are licensed Credit Brokers.*

MANAGING YOUR MONEY

---

**Leven Financial Services** cfb
Corporation of Finance Brokers Limited

**Head Office: 9 Albert Road, Middlesbrough, Cleveland TS1 1PQ**

- Life Assurance — Tax Planning — Investments
- Personal & Corporate Pension Provisions
- Commercial & Business Loans Available
- Personal Finance — Loans Secured on Property
- Mortgages & Remortgages at lower than Building Society Rates — Subject to Status
    (written details available on request)

## TEL (0642) 241461

Also at: Newcastle 091-232 1903  Carlisle 0699 2209
And Blackpool 0253 899478

Appointed Representative of  **GRE Guardian Royal Exchange**  **Lautro**

---

make sure you know exactly how much it is going to cost you. Watch out for something called the APR. This stands for the *Annual Percentage Rate* of charge. Under the Consumer Credit Act, you have the right to know the true cost of borrowing, or APR. If it isn't displayed ask what it is. The APR gives you the true rate of interest and allows you to compare different types of loan. For example, using the APR you can tell whether it is cheaper to borrow on your credit card at an interest rate of 1.75 per cent a month or with a bank personal loan with a flat rate of interest of 15 per cent.

### Where to borrow?

BANK CREDIT CARDS
Barclaycard, Trustcard and Access are the main bank credit cards. Barclaycard and Trustcard are part of the worldwide Visa system, with similar cards issued by other banks throughout the world, including, in the UK, the National Girobank, the Bank of Scotland, the Co-operative Bank and the Chase Manhattan. Access is the card issued by Lloyds, Midland, National Westminster, and the Royal Bank of Scotland.

To get any of these cards you fill in an application form. If you are accepted the card is issued free. You can apply even if you don't have an account with the bank.

When you get your card you are given a *credit limit*, which is the amount of money you can borrow with your card. Barclaycard's average credit limit at the end of 1987 was £895, but it could be as little as £100. The credit card companies say there is no upper limit.

The credit card company sends you a statement each month. This shows an amount, if any, carried forward from the previous month, plus the interest, and any purchases you made during the month. You are then faced with several choices. You can pay off the whole amount. Or you can pay off just some of it. You must always send them something. If you make a partial payment, it mustn't be less than the minimum amount shown on the statement which is set at 5 per cent of the outstanding account. Bank credit cards are good value if you clear the account every month. This way you pay no interest and if you time your purchases right you get up to 56 days' free credit.

If you want to repay the loan over a longer period, bank credit cards usually cost more than an overdraft or a bank personal loan. They have the advantage of convenience. Once you have the card, the credit is there waiting to be used, so long as you don't blot your copy book.

The Co-operative Bank encourage their customers to save with their Visa card – they pay you interest if your account is in credit.

CHARGE CARDS

The two main charge cards are American Express and Diners Club. To get a card you fill in an application form rather as if you were applying for a credit card. There is an annual subscription and unlike bank credit cards there is no extended credit – you must clear the account each month. There is no interest charge and no credit limit. The cards are only of much use if you do a lot of travelling and need to pay for expensive airline tickets and hotels. In these circumstances they can be a convenient way of paying big bills. If you use them for business travel etc, get your company to pay your annual subscription.

STORE CREDIT CARDS

Many chain and department stores now operate their own credit cards. Remember, they are a way of getting you to spend more than you want in their shop.

Store credit cards work either like a bank credit card or on a

MANAGING YOUR MONEY

# HAMILTON
## FINANCIAL GROUP LTD.
### FINANCE

**MORTGAGES**

**RE-MORTGAGES**
(for Home Improvements and Capital Raising)

**COMMERCIAL MORTGAGES**

**MARINE MORTGAGES**

**HIRE PURCHASE**
Motor Cars, Commercial Vehicles, Heavy Plant Machinery

**LEASING from £500**
Office Equipment, Computers, Security Systems,
Catering Equipment, Cars & Commercial Vehicles,
Light Plant Machinery etc.

**PERSONAL LOANS**
Holidays, Kitchens, House Furnishings, Home Improvements

**22 Victoria Avenue Whitehead Carrickfergus Co. Antrim BT38 9QF**
Telephone Whitehead (09603) 73561 (4 lines) FAX: (09603) 78223

**1st Floor 4 Shipquay Street Londonderry BT48 6DN**
Telephone Londonderry (0504) 371646 (3 lines) FAX: (0504) 371645

**11a Dobbin Street, Armagh BT61 7QQ**
Telephone Armagh (0861) 527591 (3 lines)

In Association with:
**PB Leasing Limited**

Agents for:
**HALIFAX**

revolving system. With the revolving system, you agree to pay a regular amount into the scheme each month, usually by banker's order. In return you can borrow up to 12, 20 or 24 times your monthly payment. So if you agree to pay in £10 a month and you can borrow up to 20 times your monthly payment, the card gives you the right to spend £200 in the store.

Unless you are absolutely sure you can keep your card in credit, avoid store credit cards, especially those based on a revolving system. The interest rate on store cards is usually higher than for a bank credit card or a bank personal loan. And there are very few stores which pay you interest if your account with them goes into credit. You may want to make an exception for those stores which don't take bank credit cards, such as Marks & Spencer.

Look out for special promotions. Stores sometimes offer interest-free credit deals. But first check you can't buy the item cheaper elsewhere. And a few stores, notably John Lewis, still offer a charge card, which doesn't cost anything to join, and doesn't charge interest.

BANK REVOLVING CREDIT SCHEMES
These work in the same way as some store credit cards, but they offer a better deal. The interest rate is lower than bank credit cards. The amount you can borrow is normally 30 times the monthly payment, and you do earn interest if your account goes into the black. You get a cheque book instead of a credit card, and you are charged each time you write a cheque. So watch out; if you write a lot of cheques, it puts up the cost of borrowing.

BANK OVERDRAFTS
An overdraft is the facility to borrow on your bank current account. But there are overdrafts and overdrafts. You will be charged a high rate of interest if you overdraw without the permission of your bank manager.

On the other hand, an overdraft which you have agreed with your bank manager is one of the cheapest ways of borrowing money.

Some banks now operate a sort of half-way house between an unauthorised and an agreed overdraft. If you habitually overdraw at the end of each month, your bank manager may offer you a credit limit up to which you can overdraw. The rate of interest is pitched mid-way between an unauthorised and an agreed overdraft. Resist this hard sell. Either stop overdrawing or arrange a proper overdraft.

If you run an overdraft, you must think carefully about the way you use your current account. When you overdraw you get clobbered for bank charges each time you write a cheque or make a

# LOW COST BANK LOAN

## PRESTBURY SECURITIES PERSONAL LOAN PORTFOLIO

- £2,000-£50,000 ANY PURPOSE
- NO FEES — GUARANTEED
- FREE LIFE INSURANCE
- HEALTHY REDUNDANCY COVER
- SELF EMPLOYED WITHOUT ACCOUNTS
- NO EMPLOYER CONTACT
- NO INTERVIEW
- EARLY SETTLEMENT DISCOUNTS

Whatever the purpose or amount you require Prestbury Securities will aim to provide it.

You are free to borrow up to 90% of the value of your property less any outstanding mortgage, subject to having sufficient income to meet all your commitments.

Use your loan anyway you wish, consolidate your existing commitments and reduce your outgoings, home improvements, school fees — the choice is yours.

YOU WILL BE SURPRISED HOW LOW OUR RATES ARE.

### TALK TO THE PROFESSIONALS IN PERSONAL FINANCE

## 0477-5596/7

**ANYTIME 9 AM-7 PM MON-FRI OR RETURN THE COUPON**

PRESTBURY SECURITIES (LICENSED CREDIT BROKERS)
CHAPEL HOUSE, NEWCASTLE ROAD, ARCLID, SANDBACH,
CHESHIRE CW11 0UE

---

**PS** PRESTBURY SECURITIES

POST TODAY TO: Dept DMG
Prestbury Securities, Chapel House, Newcastle Road, Arclid, Sandbach, Cheshire CW11 0UE

Name ..................................................................................................

Address ...............................................................................................

..........................................................................................................

Tel ............................................. Amount required £ .........................

**LOANS SECURED ON PROPERTY — SORRY NO TENANTS**

standing order. If you are overdrawn, keep the number of cheques you write down to a minimum by using your credit card for as many of your purchases as you can.

## PERSONAL LOANS

Personal loans are available from the high street banks, building societies and finance houses. They are used for large buys like furniture and cars. You can walk into any bank, building society or finance house and ask for a personal loan, although most people ask their own bank or building society first. The loan is normally paid back with regular monthly payments over three or five years, at a fixed rate of interest.

If you want to repay the loan early, there is a formula – called the *Rule of 78* – which lenders are required by law to use when working out the value of the outstanding loan.

Personal loans work out cheaper than using your bank credit card, and may not be much more expensive than an agreed overdraft. Finance companies are often more expensive than banks and building societies.

## SECURED LOANS

Available from some banks and building societies. If you have owned your own home for some time, its value usually far exceeds your outstanding mortgage. In recognition of this, some banks and buildings societies are now prepared to use your house as security for a loan. The interest rate is lower than bank and building society personal loans and as such these loans now offer good value for money. But don't offer up your house as security to second-line banks or finance houses without being absolutely sure of what you are signing. Many of these loans are notoriously expensive, and you risk losing your house if you can't repay the loan.

## BANK ORDINARY LOANS

Bank ordinary loans aren't promoted. They are an alternative to a bank personal loan, but they are often cheaper, because the bank asks for security. Before taking out a personal loan, ask whether you can have a bank ordinary loan instead. There is no set pattern to bank ordinary loans, each one is tailormade to suit circumstances. The rate of interest usually fluctuates with changes in bank base rates.

## HIRE PURCHASE AND CREDIT SALE

Hire purchase and credit sale agreements work in the same way as personal loans, even if legally they are both very different animals.

They are not as common as they once were, although you will still find car dealers who offer hire purchase.

When you buy a car through hire purchase, the dealer asks for a deposit. This is usually a third or 20 per cent. But it could be as low as 10 per cent. Deposits are a hangover from the days when the government placed restrictions on hire purchase and credit sale agreements. Don't always assume that the interest rate is high, although watch out for furniture stores who have a bad name. Always ask for the APR, and compare the rate with the alternatives. The rate of interest is fixed at the outset.

INSURANCE COMPANY LOANS

An insurance company loan can be one of the cheapest ways to borrow money. If you have a life insurance policy with a cash value, which normally means an endowment or whole-of-life policy, many insurance companies are prepared to lend you money, frequently at very reasonable rates of interest, using the policy as security. You don't need to repay the money either; the outstanding debt is normally just deducted from the policy when it matures or you decide to cash it in.

BANK GOLD CARDS

Bank gold cards are charge cards – they work like the American Express and Diners Club cards – for the super-rich. You won't get one unless you earn a lot of money. They are a status symbol but an expensive one. The annual fee for a gold card can be twice that of an ordinary charge card. There are three gold card companies: American Express issue the Lloyds and Royal Bank of Scotland cards; Mastercard operate the Midland and National Westminster schemes, while the Visa Premier card is issued by Barclays and the Bank of Scotland. All cards give you access to cheap overdrafts with the sponsoring bank. Unless you need the overdraft, these cards are an expensive luxury to be avoided.

TRADING CHECKS

A type of credit sold mainly door-to-door. You get trading checks – they have a value of anything between £5 and £50 – which you exchange for goods in shops which accept them. The checks are repaid in weekly instalments. The traditional trading check is worth £20, and is paid back over 21 weeks at £1 a week. This gives an APR of 26.2 per cent if you start repaying the loan after the first week, or 29.2 if you start repaying it as soon as you get it. Some trading checks cost more, so always check the APR.

PAWNBROKERS

Pawnbrokers lend money, usually for short periods. The loan is secured on personal valuables, known as the *pledge*, which could be anything from a gold watch to a camera. The loan is usually for six months, and the pawnbroker has the right to sell your belongings if you haven't paid back the loan after nine months. The rate of interest can be high but it may be the only place that will lend you money for just a couple of days with a minimum of fuss.

LOAN SHARKS

Loan sharks advertise extensively in the small advertisements of local newspapers. The bait is usually the lure of instant credit and no questions asked. *Avoid this type of lender at all costs.* The rate of interest is invariably high. And if you fail to keep up the payments, they lend you more, until you end up borrowing well beyond what you can possibly hope to repay. That's when they start getting heavy.

## The law on credit

Don't let the unscrupulous credit merchants get the better of you. The law on credit is governed mainly by the Consumer Credit Act 1974. The Act is run by the Office of Fair Trading, and almost anyone lending money to the public must be licensed with the Office of Fair Trading. The main exception is anyone only offering loans under £30. Anyone operating without a credit licence is breaking the law.

The Act also requires lenders to give consumers information on the true cost of borrowing so that different types of loan can be compared. If the information isn't forthcoming, you are entitled to ask for it.

LOAN REFUSAL

If you are ever refused a loan, and can't fathom out why, it could be the fault of a credit rating agency. These agencies hold vast data banks of information, which banks, stores and finance companies consult before authorising a loan. Sometimes these credit agencies get it wrong. You now have the right to ask the name of the credit rating agency, look at your file and correct any mistakes.

**Table 6.1** The cost of borrowing on 20 June 1988

| Loan source | Per cent |
|---|---|
| Bank base rate | 8.5 per cent |
| Authorised bank and building society overdrafts | 11.5–23.1 per cent |
| Unauthorised bank and building society overdrafts | 18.5–34.4 per cent |
| Bank ordinary loans | 11.5–15.5 per cent |
| Bank and building society personal loans | 18.0–22.9 per cent |
| Bank and building society secured loans | 13.0–15.0 per cent |
| Bank credit cards | 16.9–25.3 per cent |
| Store credit cards | 19.5–39.9 per cent |
| Finance company personal loans | 19–30 per cent |
| Hire purchase and credit sales | 20–42 per cent |
| Insurance policy loans | 10–16 per cent |

# 7
# INSURANCE

Who needs life insurance? The high pressure insurance sales people would sell it to anyone. Don't be taken in by their patter. It's often a big con.

So if you open your door one day to find yourself confronted by an insurance salesman, remember that he sees you as his prey. Once he has you in his sights, his sole aim is to get your signature on the dotted line and he will use every psychological trick in the sales manual to get it. You are his livelihood. All you are to him is a potential commission cheque. So don't believe him when he says you are letting down your family or passing up the investment opportunity of the decade. Manipulating your feelings is part of his stock-in-trade.

So if you are young, single and unattached, don't worry yourself into an early grave if you have escaped the attentions of the life insurance salesman. In fact count yourself lucky, because you probably don't need any.

And even if you are bowed down with family responsibilities with everyone from granny to the budgie depending on your pay packet, don't panic. Shop around and look for cheap, no frills policies. Search out the policies which offer such good value for money that no high pressure salesman can afford to sell them.

The life insurance men say that life insurance is never bought, it is always sold. It's their way of justifying the often appalling behaviour of insurance sales people who often end up selling the wrong policies to the wrong people.

It's a pity because life insurance really is a useful way of protecting families from the financial hardship which can follow someone's early death. In this case a little bit of knowledge is entirely a good thing. Never mind all that daunting small print in the policy document, the essentials of life insurance are not difficult and they are worth acquiring.

Life assurance divides neatly into two sorts. There are policies which are really regular savings plans in disguise. And there are policies which pay out only when you die.

There was a time when savings plans were a good deal. But in 1984 the government removed their one big attraction: tax relief on the premiums. Now there are better ways to piggy bank your money on a regular basis. See Chapter 5, *Saving*. So if anyone offers to sell you something they call a with-profits endowment plan or a unit-linked savings plan, show them the door.

Don't be so hasty in dismissing the other kind of life insurance – the sort which pays your family something when you die. If others depend on your income, you ought to think of taking some out.

## How much insurance do you need?

Your first task is taking stock. Don't rush it – you might end up with more insurance than you actually need.

You need to know two things: 1. The size of your income gap or how much it would cost to maintain your family's standard of living if you weren't there bringing in the pay packet. 2. The size of the capital gap or the lump sum which they would need to repay debts and replace things, like cars which went with you and your job.

Take a fine-tooth comb through the family budget. Use the budget planner in Chapter 4, *Budgeting* to help you. There are the things we all have to pay: rent or mortgage; the bills: rates, gas, electricity and telephone. These will stay much the same whether or not you are there. Then there is essential spending on food and clothes, which will be less, with one less body to clothe and feed. Deduct too all your personal expenses – your pocket money, your hobbies, the cost of travelling to work.

But remember, some items may be more expensive. Do you have an office car? Does your firm pay for your petrol? If they do, you will need to provide a lump sum for buying a car, and more for running it.

Even if you do nothing, your family won't be entirely penniless without you. If you are a married man, your wife might get a State Widow's Pension. This is money you can only count on lasting if your children are under 19 or your wife is over 40 when you die.

INSURANCE

## BUSINESS & FAMILY SERVICES

Specialist Financial Advisers
and
Mortgage Consultants

**Mortgage Guarantee Card**

**100% MORTGAGES     95% RE-MORTGAGES**

- INVESTMENTS
- LIFE ASSURANCE
- MOTOR ● HOUSE
- PENSIONS
- COMMERCIAL

154 QUEENSWAY
TOWN CENTRE
BILLINGHAM TS23 2NT
TEL: STOCKTON 360050

---

## PINHEY BARNES & CO
### INSURANCE BROKERS

BROKERS REGISTRATION COUNCIL: INSURANCE
REGULATED FOR INVESTMENT BUSINESS

*A personal and professional service*

**LIFE ASSURANCE ★ LIFE ASSURANCE BONDS**

**UNIT TRUSTS ★ PENSIONS**

**TELEPHONE: FELIXSTOWE (0394) 277677**

94, HAMILTON ROAD
FELIXSTOWE
SUFFOLK
IP11 7AD

MEMBER OF
**BIIBA**
BRITISH INSURANCE & INVESTMENT
BROKERS ASSOCIATION

MANAGING YOUR MONEY

Food for thought from..................

# D. F. PANTRY

friendly advice on:

- investments
- pensions
- life assurance
- mortgages
- retirement planning

### D. F. PANTRY ACII

Independent Financial Adviser
FREEPOST (BS4164)
101 Whiteladies Road
Clifton, Bristol BS8 2PE

Tel: (0272) 744138

INDEPENDENT FINANCIAL ADVISER

A FIMBRA MEMBER

Otherwise Widow's Pension comes to a grinding halt after the first six months.

If you pay into your company's pension scheme, now is a good time to grapple with the small print in the handbook. As you will discover, pensions are still very much a man's world. Most company pension schemes pay a widow's pension if a male employee dies before he retires. But there still aren't many schemes where husbands automatically get a pension from their wives' pension scheme.

Now you have the measure of the income gap. You know how much it would cost to run your family and how much they would stand to gain by your untimely death. The difference is what you should be thinking of covering with insurance.

## Family income plans

The best and cheapest way to provide a steady regular income is with a family income plan. With this kind of life insurance you undertake to pay the insurance company a regular premium (normally every month) for a predetermined number of years.

If you die before you finish paying the premiums the insurance company pays your family a regular monthly income until that predetermined number of years is up. The policies are often arranged to finish when your youngest child comes of age at 18. The policy is cheap because it only pays out if you die. You don't get your money back if you are still alive when the policy ends.

You can arrange for the income to last longer if you think your children are destined for higher education, or your other half will still need an income once the children are out of the way.

To avoid the ravages of inflation, it is a good idea to buy a policy where the income increases by a certain percentage each year. You can ask for any figure you like, but 5 per cent seems a sensible figure to aim for. And how much will this set you back? Shop around for the cheapest premiums. But if you are around 30 you shouldn't pay more than £5 a month for a policy which lasts 18 years and pays an income of £5,000 a year if you die before you reach 48. Ten years later the risk of dying over the next 18 years before 58 is that much higher. But still you shouldn't have to pay more than £10 a month for a policy paying the same income of £5,000 a year.

For a policy which increases at 5 per cent a year, the premium for a 30-year old rises to around £7 a month, and for a 40-year old to around £15.

If you are the one that stays at home it's worth insuring your life

MANAGING YOUR MONEY

# HAMILTON
## FINANCIAL GROUP LTD.
**INSURANCE**

**LIFE ASSURANCE**
**SAVINGS SCHEMES**

**INVESTMENTS**
**UNIT TRUSTS**

**PERSONAL PENSION PLANS**
**GROUP PERSONAL PENSION PLANS**
**COMPANY PENSION PLANS**

**PERSONAL PERMANENT HEALTH INSURANCE**
**GROUP PERMANENT HEALTH INSURANCE**

**TAX PLANNING**

**FINANCIAL PLANNING FOR THE FUTURE**

22 Victoria Avenue Whitehead Carrickfergus Co. Antrim BT38 9QF
Telephone Whitehead (09603) 73561 (4 lines) FAX: (09603) 78223

1st Floor 4 Shipquay Street Londonderry BT48 6DN
Telephone Londonderry (0504) 371646 (3 lines) FAX: (0504) 371645

11a Dobbin Street, Armagh BT61 7QQ
Telephone Armagh (0861) 527591 (3 lines)

**SUN LIFE unit services**
— Applied to Lautro

Hamilton Financial Group Ltd. is an Appointed Representative of Sun Life Unit Services Limited for the purposes only of making introductions for Life Assurance, Pensions and Unit Trust Contracts to companies in the Sun Life Group.

Agents for:

**HALIFAX**

too, with a family income plan. Small children need full-time care, and nannies, or even child-minders, don't come cheap. Sit down and work out how much it would cost if you had to pay someone to stay at home. The size of the bill will probably come as a shock.

## How much lump sum insurance?

Now you know the size of your income gap, think about providing a lump sum to repay loans, or replace assets which might be linked to your job. Make a list of what you owe the banks, building societies, credit card and finance companies.

If you have an insurance-linked mortgage and you die early, your family gets a lump sum which is large enough to repay the mortgage.

If you don't have an insurance-linked mortgage, your family gets nothing if you die, and you should take out separate insurance.

There is a cheap type of insurance – ask for *mortgage protection insurance* – which provides a lump sum to repay the outstanding mortgage should you die early. The policy is cheap because the sum needed to repay the mortgage goes down over the years.

Premiums on a mortgage protection policy shouldn't cost you more than about £4 a month if you are age 30 and have a £30,000 mortgage repayable over 25 years. If you take out the same mortgage at age 40, aim to pay premiums of not more than £10 a month.

Before buying lump sum insurance, check that you aren't already insured. Some banks add on free life insurance, or offer it as an optional extra, when you take out a loan. If you do need insurance, the best types are term insurance and whole-of-life.

How much insurance you need depends on the generosity of your employers. Some pension schemes provide a lump sum of two or two-and-a-half times your yearly salary, which is paid to your family if you die early. And if you are in a pension scheme there is normally some sort of widow's pension. And as we have seen there is a state widow's pension for wives over 40.

The cheapest way of providing a lump sum is to use *term insurance*. This is similar to a family income plan, except it pays a lump sum rather than a regular income if you die early. In insurance jargon the length of the policy is called the *term*. So if you take out a policy with a 30-year term, it only pays out if you die during the next 30 years. If you die the day after the policy expires your family gets nothing.

This makes the premiums relatively cheap. A man age 30 taking out a policy which would pay £100,000 if he died within the next 35 years to retirement should shop around for a policy which doesn't

## Arthur Marsh & Son
(Insurance Brokers) Ltd.

*All classes of Insurance arranged with helpful service*

MEMBER OF
**BIIBA**
BRITISH INSURANCE & INVESTMENT BROKERS' ASSOCIATION

1286 Uxbridge Road
Hayes End
Hayes
Middlesex
UB4 8JG

01-573 7060
01-573 7586
Fax: 01-569 1102

# WANTAGE INSURANCE

**AUTHORISED INVESTMENT BROKERS SERVING**
## OXFORDSHIRE
**NO FEES CHARGED**
**CALL US TODAY**
Registered Insurance Brokers

INDEPENDENT FINANCIAL ADVISER

A FIMBRA MEMBER

15 Market Place
Wantage
Tel: 02357 68850/68896

cost more than £27 a month. A 40-year old taking out a similar policy to retirement should aim to pay no more than £42 a month.

You could also take out a *whole-of-life policy*, but this would be an expensive option. This is a hybrid policy with elements of both protection and savings. With a whole-of-life policy, your family always gets something. If you decide to insure yourself for £100,000 your family gets the money whether you die the following day, or 50 years later. With most companies you carry on paying premiums until you die, with others the premiums stop at age 80.

Whole-of-life is more expensive than term insurance. A 30-year old pays around £75 a month for a policy paying out £100,000, a 40-year old around £130 a month.

To summarise. If you have a family, you probably need life insurance. Go for:

1. Family income plan: to pay a yearly income if you die before your children are ready to leave home.
2. Mortgage protection policy: to provide a lump sum for repaying any outstanding mortgage loan, if you don't have an insurance-linked mortgage.
3. Term insurance or whole-of-life insurance: to provide a lump sum to repay loans and replace things like cars if these go with the job.

## What else is on offer?

There are other forms of life insurance. Don't let any zealous sales person sell you one without taking a critical look at what is on offer.

### INCREASABLE, RENEWABLE TERM

With increasable, renewable term you can take out small amounts of insurance for short periods. You then have the option to increase the amount and the term, regardless of your state of health: a cheap form of life insurance. You are basically insuring yourself against the possibility that you fall ill and can't get life insurance.

### WITH-PROFITS ENDOWMENT INSURANCE

With-profits endowment insurance is a savings contract. You agree to save a regular amount for at least 10 years. The policy increases in value and earns bonuses linked to the profits of the life insurance company. A safe investment, but dull. Poor value if you cash it in early. If you die before the end of the policy, your family gets the *sum insured*. This is often the greater of the cash-in value of the policy or all the premiums due under the policy if it had run its course.

## MANAGING YOUR MONEY

# SAVE MONEY ON YOUR MOTOR INSURANCE

Save money on your motor insurance by dealing direct with The Insurance Service. It could save you pounds!

We guarantee to freeze the price you pay for two years. Yes, the price you pay this year is the price you pay next year! Even if you make a claim!

We've over a thousand Recommended Repairers, who don't need authorisation before they start work on your car. So you can get back on the road faster.

Getting a free quote is as easy as dialling our number. And you can be covered before you've put the phone down.

Even if your renewal is months away, call us now and we'll send you a quotation nearer the time.

> Just say YES to these 4 questions, and you could be saying yes to a cheaper premium:
> 1. Are all drivers aged between 21 and 74, and have held a full UK licence for 3 years or more?
> 2. Are all drivers accident and conviction free for the last three years?
> 3. Are you entitled to at least 50% no claims bonus on your next renewal?
> 4. Is your car a family saloon, hatchback or estate car?

# 0272·232·232

Remember: You are under no obligation to accept our quote. The Insurance Service plc is a subsidiary of Cavendish Insurance plc, a member of the Association of British Insurers and the Insurance Ombudsman Bureau.

---

**PLEASE SEND ME A FREE QUOTATION.**   Offer only available mainland UK.

MAIN DRIVER   PLEASE USE BLOCK CAPITALS
Mr/Mrs/Miss   Surname   Forenames
Address
   Postcode
Date of Birth   Phone No. (Day)   (Evening)
Other drivers: (Please include all drivers in your household.)
Full Name   Date of Birth
Full Name   Date of Birth
Please only send this coupon if you can answer YES to these four questions. (Tick box)
Are you entitled to at least 50% no claims bonus at your next renewal date? (Written confirmation of this will be required).
Are all drivers aged between 21 and 74, and have held a full U.K. licence for 3 years or more?
Are all drivers accident and conviction free for the last three years or more? (Up to 2 speeding/parking convictions don't count).
Is the car you wish to insure a family saloon, hatch-back or estate. NOT a van or high performance car?
Quotation required: Comprehensive |   Third Party, Fire & Theft
Car Make   Model   Type (L.GL etc)   Engine Size (cc)   Year
Registration No.   Expiry Date of Present Policy   Annual Mileage (approx)
Garaged at night Yes | No |   Car Usage: Social, Domestic & Pleasure |   Travel to work |   Business |

Please Post to: THE INSURANCE SERVICE PLC, FREEPOST, BRISTOL BS1 3YS
or Phone 0272 232 232 (8am-8pm Mon.-Fri. 9am-Noon Sat.)

**DMM 20**   " **THE INSURANCE SERVICE** "

## UNIT-LINKED SAVINGS PLANS

These plans are similar to with-profits endowment plans, but the premiums are invested in units in a fund. You can keep track of your investment by checking the price of the fund in the newspaper.

The value of the policy depends on the success of the fund. The results are less predictable than a with-profits endowment policy. If the policy comes to an end while the stock market is riding high the return will be good, but it may do badly if it coincides with a time when the stock market is in the doldrums. There are better ways to invest in the Stock Exchange.

## MAXIMUM INVESTMENT PLANS

Similar to unit-linked savings plans. A high proportion of each premium goes towards buying investments, a very low proportion is used to buy life insurance. They normally run for 10 years, but there is no tax to pay if they are cashed in after at least three-quarters of their term. This makes them a useful tax shelter for higher-rate taxpayers.

Now if you fall under the proverbial bus, you have the peace of mind of knowing that your family won't be plagued with money worries. It's worth giving your insurance policies the once over every couple of years. Inflation and rising living standards soon eat into the best-laid plans, and unless you have fallen seriously ill in the meantime, it is an easy matter to top up your policies.

# Sickness insurance

Have you ever thought what would happen if you fell ill and couldn't work? It's a fact that young people are much more likely to fall seriously ill than die young. And yet sickness insurance or *permanent health insurance*, as the insurance people often call it, still hasn't caught on.

Sickness insurance pays you an income if you fall ill and can't work, or have to take a pay cut. The premiums are paid until normal retirement age, and if you make a claim, the benefit stops at retirement age as well.

How much money would you and your family have to live on if you had to stop work?

Your employer must pay you at least the minimum laid down in the state Statutory Sick Pay scheme during the first 28 weeks of any absence from work due to ill health. Statutory Sick Pay depends on how much you earn, but the amounts are quite small, and well below the average working wage. From 6 April 1988 Statutory Sick Pay is

£49.20 a week if you earn more than £79.50 a week and £34.25 if you earn between £41 and £79.50 a week. If you earn less than £41 a week, you get nothing.

There are two useful DHSS leaflets on the Statutory Sick Pay scheme: **NI.208:** *National Insurance Contribution Rates and Statutory Sick Pay Rates* and **NI.244:** *Check Your Right to Statutory Sick Pay*, both available from local DHSS offices.

None the less you still may not need any extra sickness insurance. Check what your employer has on offer. Good pension schemes give early retirement pensions so find out how much you would get. Most employers keep you on the payroll on full pay for between three and six months if you fall ill. A few offer comprehensive sick pay schemes and continue to pay you a proportion of your salary even if you never go back to work.

Check what you would get if you fell ill and had to take a long period off work. Only think about taking out sickness insurance if there is a gap between what you get from the state and your employer and what you need to live on.

The self-employed who don't have the protection of an employer almost certainly need some sickness insurance.

With sickness insurance there are several variations on a theme. You can take out a policy where the premiums stay the same until you retire. You can have a policy where the benefit stays the same or increases by, say, 5 per cent a year. There are also policies where the premium increases each year, as does the benefit.

You can keep down the cost of sickness insurance by going for a policy which doesn't pay anything in the early days or months of any illness. For the self-employed, who lose pay from the day they go sick, this may not be possible, unless they have savings to draw on. But if your employer pays you during the first six months of any illness, you can take out a sickness insurance policy which only starts paying you an income when your employer stops.

If you are a man age 30 you should be able to find a sickness insurance policy which costs around £10 a month for a benefit of £10,000 a year, if you can delay making a claim for six months. And if you are 40 you shouldn't have to pay more than £16 a month for a similar policy.

Women get a raw deal on sickness insurance. The insurance companies say that women are a worse risk than men, they fall ill more often and for longer periods. Women find they have to pay from a third to half as much again as men for sickness insurance. A self-employed woman dentist recently took her insurance company to court to challenge the practice, but the judge ruled that the

INSURANCE

# McQUITTY/ROSS    Royal Life Estates

## *1*

## NEW BOARD APPOINTMENTS

**McQUITTY/ROSS**

**FOR SALE**
VIEWING BY APPOINTMENT

Royal Life Estates   NEWTOWNARDS 813808
INC: A.B.YOUNG & CO.

**McQUITTY/ROSS**

**UNDER OFFER**

Royal Life Estates   NEWTOWNARDS 813808
INC: A.B.YOUNG & CO.

**McQUITTY/ROSS**

**SOLD**
SUBJECT TO CONTRACT

Royal Life Estates   NEWTOWNARDS 813808
INC: A.B.YOUNG & CO.

**THE 3 STAGES OF SUCCESS
McQUITTY/ROSS STYLE**

Depend on McQuitty/Ross.
**OFFICES PROVINCEWIDE**

MANAGING YOUR MONEY

# LAWSONS

Specialists in all forms of Insurance including:-

★ MOTOR  ★ HOUSEHOLD
★ HOLIDAY  ★ PERSONAL

WE ARE MEMBERS OF THE BRITISH INSURANCE AND INVESTMENT BROKERS ASSOCIATION WITH A PROFESSIONAL BACKGROUND DATING BACK TO 1960

CONTACT:

**D. LAWSON & SON (INSURANCES) LTD**

1227/31, Warwick Road, Acocks Green
Birmingham, Tel: 021-707 1644
or 1219 Pershore Road, Stirchley
Birmingham, Tel: 021-459 1331

ACCESS AND VISA ACCEPTED

## FAMILY PROTECTION PLANS

PENSIONS SPECIALISTS —
SEE US BEFORE YOU ACT

VERY LOW INTEREST MORTGAGES ARRANGED

100% MORTGAGES READILY AVAILABLE

FREE SURVEY FEES SCHEME

**SHAW HEATH INSURANCE BROKERS**
32 SHAW HEATH
STOCKPORT, CHESHIRE SK3 8BD
061-477 6677/7588

**WE ARE INDEPENDENT FINANCIAL ADVISERS**

insurance company was justified in charging higher premiums.

## Buildings and contents insurance

Death and sickness are the major disasters which can hit a family. But a fire, a flood or a burglary, apart from the horror of the event, can spell severe financial hardship too.

Everyone is wise to insure their belongings. If you own your home, you should insure the building as well. This will be obligatory if you have a mortgage. Buildings insurance covers the building itself and all its permanent fixtures and fittings.

For example, it pays up if your chip pan catches fire and ruins your kitchen, or if burst pipes mean your basement has to be replastered. It may also pay up if you burn a hole in the work top in your fitted kitchen and have to replace it.

When you take out a mortgage, building societies usually insist you take out buildings insurance through them. Most people do this without questioning the practice. Remember, your building society should offer you the choice of three insurance companies and you still have the right to choose your own company.

Always make sure you have enough insurance. You need to find out how much it would cost to rebuild your house. Don't make the mistake of insuring it for the price you paid for it. This may not be the same as the cost of rebuilding. The Association of British Insurers (ABI) publish a useful booklet to help you work out how much it would cost to rebuild your house. You can get the booklet from ABI, Aldermary House, Queen Street, London EC4N 1TT.

There are several points to watch with buildings insurance. In some areas you may have to shop around to find an insurance company willing to insure your house against subsidence. And you will always have to pay the first £500 of any subsidence claim.

If you have a habit of breaking things which are covered by the policy, ask for accidental cover. It costs more but it means you can claim for that broken window, kicked-in door, or burned work top.

Now you need to insure what's in your house. With house contents insurance there is a lot of money to be saved by shopping around. But before you start comparing policies it is important to understand the difference between those which offer only indemnity terms and those which offer new-for-old.

- With *indemnity* terms your contents are insured for what they cost less an amount for wear and tear. If you make a claim you won't get enough money to replace everything new.
- When you make a claim with a *new-for-old* policy you get what it

costs to buy things new.

Expensive items like jewellery, furs or cameras, should be listed separately. You can ask for *all risks* cover for those items which you regularly take out of the house.

The cost of house contents insurance depends on where you live. It's more expensive in those areas which have the highest level of insurance claims. However, insurance companies don't always agree on which areas carry the highest risk, so if you are in a high risk area with one insurance company, don't always assume that all insurance companies put a high villainy rating on your street.

---

# INSURANCE & MORTGAGE SERVICES LTD

## WE HAVE THE MORTGAGE TO SUIT YOUR NEEDS

- 100% MORTGAGES
- REMORTGAGES
- LOW START SCHEMES
- NON STATUS MORTGAGES
- COMMERCIAL MORTGAGES

### CONTACT US TODAY FOR A COMPUTERISED QUOTATION

*WE WILL ONLY BE TOO PLEASED TO HELP*

17 BALLS POND ROAD
LONDON N1 4AX

249-7837
249-8475

# INSURANCE

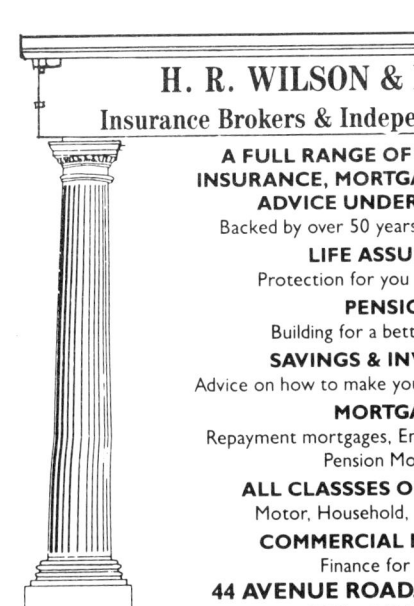

## H. R. WILSON & PARTNERS LTD
### Insurance Brokers & Independent Financial Advisers

**A FULL RANGE OF INDEPENDENT INSURANCE, MORTGAGE & FINANCIAL ADVICE UNDER ONE ROOF**

Backed by over 50 years of personal service

**LIFE ASSURANCE**
Protection for you and your family

**PENSIONS**
Building for a better retirement

**SAVINGS & INVESTMENT**
Advice on how to make your money work for you

**MORTGAGES**
Repayment mortgages, Endowment Mortgages, Pension Mortgages

**ALL CLASSSES OF INSURANCE**
Motor, Household, Commercial etc

**COMMERCIAL MORTGAGES**
Finance for business

**44 AVENUE ROAD, HARTLEPOOL**
**TEL: 0429 279826**
also at Stockton & Peterlee

BIIBA

---

| PLATT (LIFE & PENSIONS) LTD | KEITH M PLATT (I.B) LTD |
|---|---|
| 17 Sun Lane WAKEFIELD | 24 Trinity Church Gate WAKEFIELD |
| (0924) 378755 | (0924) 369898 |
| | |
| Pensions - of every kind: | Public & Private Hire |
| Self Employed/Employee | Private Motor Car |
| Company Schemes | Personal Accident/Sickness Insurance |
| Individual/Self Administered | Household Insurance |
| Pension Mortgages for the discerning individual | Public Liability |
| Investments | Employers Liability |
| Lump sum/Monthly | Commercial risks of all kinds |
| Term Assurance | Marine |
| All enquires to Mr Brian Bell | All enquires to Mrs Rosemary Ashplant |

| WAKEFIELD | DUNDEE | GLASGOW | BLACKPOOL |
|---|---|---|---|
| (0924) 369898 | (0382) 810863 | (041) 221 7650 | (0253) 27697 |
| (0924) 378755 | (0382) 811813 | (041) 221 5686 | |
| Tom McFadden | Janet Simpson | Dave McDonald | Gerry Shiers |

## UNION ALLIED
### (INSURANCE SERVICES)

**FOR THE INDIVIDUAL:**    MORTGAGES
                                      PENSIONS
                                      LIFE ASSURANCE

**FOR THE EMPLOYER/
UNION REPRESENTATIVE:** GROUP PENSIONS
                                      GROUP PERMANENT
                                      HEALTH
                                      GROUP LIFE
                                      ASSURANCE

**APPOINTED FINANCIAL
ADVISER**
LONDON AND MANCHESTER
ASSURANCE COMPANY LTD
LAUTRO

**TEL LEEDS 760014
OR
FREEPOST LS11 9YY**

---

## IT PAYS TO CHOOSE WISELY!

**WE SELECT THE VERY BEST POLICIES, SO WHATEVER YOU NEED TO INSURE**

FIMBRA MEMBER

- Motor
- Household
- Life
- Pensions
- Health

- Investments
- Mortgages
- Liability
- Commercial
- Travel

INDEPENDENT FINANCIAL ADVISER

INDEPENDENT FINANCIAL ADVISOR
PHONE US NOW ON

**01-864 9869**                       (24 HRS) MON-FRID 9-5

**A. HAMPTON & CO**
(REGISTERED INSURANCE BROKERS)
198 Alexandra Ave, South Harrow, Middx

INSURANCE

# Pilling & Company

**SUCCESSFUL FUND MANAGEMENT
FOR THE PRIVATE INVESTOR**

In 1987 when the majority of managed insurance funds showed losses the investment bond funds managed by **Pilling & Company** on behalf of other investment advisers rose by between 27% to 45%.

If you are dissatisfied with your current adviser or do not have one then contact **Robin Hodgson**.

12 St. Ann's Square, Manchester. M2 7HT

061-832 6581

Members of THE STOCK EXCHANGE

# DON'T SIGN ANYTHING UNLESS YOU SEE THIS SIGN.

(FIMBRA MEMBER)

Only an Independent Financial Adviser
works for you in recommending the best life
insurance, pensions or unit trusts on the market.
To be sure you get the best deal, contact us.

## Williamson Moore (Investments) Ltd.

The Commodore Suite
Birdham Yacht Club
CHICHESTER PO20 7BB
Tel: 0243 511301

MANAGING YOUR MONEY

*James Fernley & Partners (Life & Pensions)* have been established over 27 years and are Independent Financial Planning Consultants & Insurance Brokers.

Giving a Personal Professional Service & advice to clients on Mortgages, Private and Commercial, Life Assurance, Personal & Group Pensions, Annuities, Unit Trusts, Unit Linked Bonds and Private Health and Loss of Income Insurances.

Telephone for advice Today.

## JAMES FERNLEY & PARTNERS
**(Life & Pensions)**
35 Frogmore, Park Street, St Albans, Hertfordshire AL2 2JT
**PARK STREET (0727) 73500**

# Williams & Sherlock

## INSURANCE SERVICES

### MORTGAGE, FINANCE INVESTMENT & INSURANCE SPECIALISTS
### COMMERCIAL LOANS REQUEST ALSO DEALT WITH

Appointed Representative of **Guardian Royal Exchange**

22 UPPER PARK STREET
LLANELLI
DYFED
Tel: 0554 776 048

7a STEPNEY ROAD
BURRY PORT
DYFED
Tel: 05546 3765

*Agents for Nationwide Anglia Building Society*

---

## P. J. WALLER
## INSURANCE CONSULTANT

### SPECIALIST IN ALL INSURANCE

- COMMERCIAL    • MOTOR    • LIFE
- PENSIONS    • PERSONAL    • INVESTMENTS
- 100% MORTGAGES S.T.S.

WRITTEN DETAILS ON REQUEST

FOR FURTHER INFORMATION
TELEPHONE NOW

## NORWICH (0603) 619370
### 62 LIVINGSTONE STREET, NORWICH

(FIMBRA MEMBER)    ALLIANCE ✚ LEICESTER
BUILDING SOCIETY

# Godwins for independent expert advice on all aspects of personal financial planning.

**Head Office GODWINS Ltd
Briarcliff House, Kingsmead
Farnborough, Hants GU14 7TE**

and at:

GODWINS (CENTRAL): Farnborough, Sevenoaks.

GODWINS (MIDLANDS & WEST): Birmingham, Bristol, Cardiff, Cheltenham, Northampton, Nottingham.

GODWINS (NORTH): Belfast, Dundee, Edinburgh, Glasgow, Harrogate, Kendal, Leeds, Manchester, Newcastle.

GODWINS (SOUTH): Farnborough, St. Albans, London, Norwich

GODWINS (SOUTH WEST): Crediton, Plymouth, Portsmouth, Torquay, Truro.

FIMBRA MEMBER

*Godwins*

# 8
# GOING ABROAD

Everyone knows the damage caused by Christmas and the winter sales. They leave a trail of wreckage in your finances. And just as you resolve to save more and spend less in the new year, those tempting holiday brochures beckon you from the windows of so many travel agents.

A summer holiday is a big drain on the family budget, which of course is no reason not to take one. A holiday for a family of four in a popular resort in Spain, could easily cost a tenth of the average family income.

Going abroad isn't necessarily any more expensive than taking a holiday at home, but it does need more planning. There are decisions to be made. How do you take your money? If you go with a tour operator is the insurance cover they offer worth taking out? If you take your car, do you need any extra insurance?

Start planning early. Don't leave it all to the last minute rush which is always inevitable however well you plan your holiday. Some items can take at least a month to arrange. Even getting foreign currency from your clearing bank can take a week.

## Your holiday checklist

THREE MONTHS BEFORE YOU GO
- Think about vaccinations, especially if you are going to the Far East, India or Africa. For example, if you are going to India you will need to be vaccinated against malaria, cholera, typhoid, polio and

## MANAGING YOUR MONEY

possibly yellow fever. The vaccination for typhoid requires two injections spaced between four and six weeks apart, and that for polio requires three doses, which are spaced between four and eight weeks apart. The Department of Health and Social Security publishes two booklets in the series Travellers' Guides to Health: **SA40**, *Before you go*; and **SA41**, *While you are away*, which are available from local DHSS offices or travel agents.

- Serious delays in obtaining passports are experienced at the time of writing. Check the situation now. If a British Visitors Passport will suffice, this can be obtained through the post office. If a full passport is essential, it saves time to deliver documents personally. See below.

### TWO MONTHS BEFORE YOU GO

- If you haven't got a passport apply for one.
- If you already have a passport, check that it is up to date.
- And if you are travelling with children, arrange to put them on your passport, or if they are likely to travel independently in the near future, say on a school trip, it might be worth getting them their own passports.
- Arrange any visas or other special travel documents which may be needed for the countries you are visiting.

### SIX WEEKS BEFORE YOU GO

- Pay the remainder of any money due to your tour operator. Most ask for a £50 deposit when you book your holiday, with the rest payable six to eight weeks before you go.
- Sort out what you want to do about holiday insurance. Don't automatically take the tour operator's insurance package. Holiday insurance covers you against a whole range of potential disasters, anything from falling ill and cancelling your holiday, to having your luggage and favourite camera stolen. Once you know how much insurance you need, you can wait a while. Holiday insurance takes two weeks at the most to arrange.
- If you are going to a Common Market country get an E111 form by filling in an application form available from your local Department of Health and Social Security. The E111 entitles you to claim treatment from the state medical service in the country where you are staying.

  The system can be extremely cumbersome to use, and you may still have to pay some of the medical bill. The form doesn't automatically give you the right to free medical treatment. For example in France, you need to find a doctor who is on the state

## GOING ABROAD

### SIMPLY A CHEAPER QUOTE!

| | |
|---|---|
| TEL. 01-502 1337 | 38 CHURCH HILL<br>LOUGHTON, ESSEX. |
| TEL. 01-558 1286 | 373 HIGH ROAD<br>LEYTON E10. |
| TEL. 01-889 3434 | 201 GREEN LANES<br>PALMERS GREEN N13 |
| ROYSTON 41186 | 57 HIGH STREET<br>ROYSTON, HERTS |
| TEL. 01-524 4974 | 2 OLD CHURCH ROAD<br>CHINGFORD E4 |
| STEVENAGE 358357 | 105 HIGH STREET<br>STEVENAGE, HERTS |

**INSTANT COVER**

## STONE MOTOR POLICIES

panel of doctors, you can't use just any doctor. And only a proportion of the bill is paid by the state. The more serious the complaint the higher the percentage.

None the less an E111 is a useful additional document. Take it along with your UK medical card. You don't need to get one each time you go abroad. It lasts until you make a claim.

- If you want to cash cheques while you are on holiday, order your Eurocheque card and Eurocheques now. The banks say they take at least three weeks to come through. With most banks you must renew your Eurocheque card every year.

A MONTH BEFORE YOU GO

- Think about car insurance. Check your car insurance is up to date. Do you need any extra insurance? In the Common Market you can drive without any extra insurance, but your cover is limited to the legal minimum required in the country you are visiting. To get fully comprehensive car insurance while you are in Europe, you need to ask your insurance company for a *continental extension*. You can also get a *Green Card*. This is your proof that your car insurance is at least up to the legal minimum required. If you drive outside the Common Market, in Scandinavia for example, a Green Card

## MANAGING YOUR MONEY

is obligatory. Why Green Card? Who knows? It's not a card, but it is green.
- Investigate car breakdown and recovery insurance. You get it from the major motoring organisations and some cross-channel ferry operators, as well as a few others. It's definitely worth considering if your car is old or unreliable. Among other things, it pays for repairing your car after a breakdown, hotel bills if you are stranded, and getting you and your family home. This kind of insurance only covers you while travelling in Europe.

TWO WEEKS BEFORE YOU GO
- Order your holiday money. You can choose between the local currency, travellers cheques, or using your cheque book, or a combination of two or more. If you live or work near a branch of Thomas Cook or American Express, they can probably give you the common European currencies and American dollars plus travellers cheques while you wait. The same may be true of large city centre branches of the big clearing banks. Most bank branches don't do foreign exchange and they have to order it. This can take a week, so give your bank plenty of notice.

Now you have your checklist, you need to know how to find the best insurance policies, and the best way to take your money.

## Holiday insurance

Holiday insurance pays your medical bills if you fall ill, and a lump sum if you are killed or injured in an accident. You are also covered if any money, luggage or valuables are lost or stolen, or if your holiday is cancelled or cut short for a reason beyond your control, such as illness or redundancy.

You can design your own package, by choosing the amount of insurance you need in each section. If you were going backpacking to the United States, you might choose high medical cover, but a small amount of cover for your luggage.

Points to watch: some companies refuse to pay up if you are being treated for a condition you already had before you went away. Choose a company which only excludes existing conditions when you travel against your doctor's advice.

If you are the active outdoor sort, check that your favourite pastime isn't excluded. Water sports and mountaineering are often not covered.

Make sure you have enough medical cover for places where the cost of medical treatment is high, as it is, for example, in the United States.

Skiing holidays are a special case. Broken limbs are two a penny on the ski slopes, so your tour operator normally only accepts your booking if you take out insurance. If you don't take out the insurance they offer, they ask you to prove that you are insured. Most tour operators offer more than adequate medical cover. Just a few don't. If you think yours doesn't, you should make your own insurance arrangements.

Some insurance companies find it cheaper to fly people home in an air taxi rather than pay the cost of foreign hospital bills. If you would prefer to be ill at home, find a company which offers such a service.

And watch out for excesses. Try to find a policy which doesn't ask you to pay the first part of any claim.

## Car breakdown and recovery insurance

As with holiday insurance, car breakdown and recovery insurance is a package and it's up to you to decide how much cover you need.

If your car breaks down, it pays for any roadside repairs. If the problem is more fundamental, it pays for towing the car to a garage, and getting it repaired, including the cost of sending spare parts from Britain. You can extend the policy to pay for hotel accommodation while your car is being repaired.

If the car can't be repaired abroad, it pays the cost of getting the car and your family home. And if you have to leave the car behind, it pays your fares when you collect it. If you fall ill and can't drive your car home, it pays the cost of a chauffeur to bring it back. It pays for legal bills if you get involved in a court case after an accident, including in most cases a free bail bond in Spain, where they are very keen on putting motoring offenders in gaol.

Read the brochure carefully. You may find you have to pay the first slice of any claim. Also the maximum claim is not always generous. If you have a taste for high living, some policies only allow you to claim a modest amount for staying in a hotel.

If you are taking your car to one of the Mediterranean islands, such as Malta, Cyprus or Crete, check that the insurance company operates its recovery service there. Some don't.

## Holiday money

There are four ways of organising your holiday money. You can use cash, Eurocheques and Postcheques, travellers cheques or credit cards, or a combination of two or more.

### CASH

Cash may be the cheapest way of taking money abroad, but it is not the safest. In the relaxed mood of a holiday, cash is easily lost or stolen.

Your holiday insurance pays out if your holiday money is lost or stolen, but the amount is usually restricted. So when on holiday, never take more cash than you are insured for.

None the less it is a good idea to take a small amount of the local currency. Most holidays start at the weekend when the banks are shut, and you need cash to tide you over the first couple of days until the banks open again.

If you take pounds sterling, it's always best to get your money changed at a branch of a large bank. This is where you are likely to get the best exchange rate and the lowest handling charge. Avoid using independent bureaux de change or those on cross channel ferries. They don't always offer the best exchange rate.

### EUROCHEQUES AND POSTCHEQUES

Eurocheques and Postcheques are now the most convenient way of arranging your holiday money in Europe. But you must remember to order them well before you go on holiday.

With a Eurocheque and a Eurocheque card you can cash a cheque on your current account at any bank in Europe which is in the Eurocheque system, and displays the Eurocheque symbol.

Postcheques and the Postcheque card provide a similar service for National Girobank customers. With a Postcheque you can cash a cheque on your Girobank account at post offices.

Eurocheques and Postcheques give you access to your bank account while you are on holiday. This is particularly useful if your monthly salary cheque goes into your account while you are away.

The banks don't automatically dole out Eurocheques and Eurocheque cards. It's your bank manager who decides. Check the bank's decision. They won't necessarily tell you if your application is turned down, and there may not be enough time to get your bank to change their mind.

Eurocheques and Postcheques may be convenient, but they aren't the cheapest way of taking money abroad. There is a yearly fee for issuing the Eurocheque card (most banks only issue them for a year). There is a flat fee each time you use a Eurocheque and a percentage handling charge levied on the value of the cheque.

The Postcheques system works out more cheaply. You pay for a book of 10 cheques whether or not you use them all. This costs not much more than a Eurocheque card. The Postcheque card is free, and the handling charge is lower.

Both systems have a major disadvantage: you don't know the exchange rate when you cash your cheque. This is because Eurocheques and Postcheques are normally written out in the local currency. So if you are in France, you ask for the amount you want in French francs; if in Spain, you ask for pesetas.

The foreign exchange calculation is only made when the cheque arrives home at your bank. This takes up to a fortnight and it has been known for people to wait up to two months. This is a distinct disadvantage if the pound falls while you wait for your cheque to go through the system. It works to your advantage, of course, if the pound is rising over the same period. However, it does stop you from shopping around the banks for the best rate of exchange, if that is how you enjoy spending your holidays.

There are some places where you are better off with Eurocheques than Postcheques. The Eurocheque system is more widespread. It covers a number of Eastern European countries (cheques here are written in US dollars rather than in the local currency) where Postcheques fear to tread.

Eurocheques can also be used in hotels, shops and restaurants displaying the Eurocheque symbol. Postcheques can only be used for drawing cash. There are even a few countries where Eurocheque cards can be used in cash dispensers.

TRAVELLERS CHEQUES

Now it is so easy to swan around Europe spending money out of your current account and not getting billed for it immediately, why bother with travellers cheques?

The banks say fewer holidaymakers now take travellers cheques to Europe although they remain popular with travellers outside Europe.

Travellers cheques are an alternative to cash. You buy them before you go on holiday. They are often minor works of art, elaborately designed, and embossed. You can use them to pay for airline tickets, hotel rooms, and in shops.

So don't dismiss travellers cheques completely out of hand. They still have their uses and not just when you travel outside Europe.

If the pound is wobbling on the world's foreign exchange markets, think about buying travellers cheques in the currency of the country you are visiting. If you give them enough notice most banks can get you travellers cheques in a wide range of currencies. There is no problem getting United States dollar travellers cheques. Others are available in Swiss and French francs, Spanish pesetas, Italian lire, and German deutschmarks.

This way you buy your foreign currency at the start of your holiday, and you don't watch the value of your holiday money decline with the exchange rate.

You will probably end up taking travellers cheques if your holiday takes you to the United States, or exotic places like India or the Far East.

Take dollar travellers cheques to the United States where they are almost as good as cash. In other parts of the world, sterling travellers cheques may be a better bet, if you expect the exchange rate to stay stable or rise. But think about taking dollar travellers cheques if you are going somewhere remote. Off the beaten tourist track, in some remote village somewhere up the Ganges, the dollar exchange rate may be the only one anyone can quote.

Play safe with travellers cheques. Follow the advice you get when you collect them. The bank or travel agent will ask you to sign every cheque before handing over the final documents. This can be a surprisingly wrist-aching job, if you have asked for your cheques to be issued in small denominations. Keep a record of the serial numbers of the cheques, and keep it separately from the cheques. Don't keep any personal identification in the same place as your travellers cheques, and keep a note of which ones you have cashed.

If your travellers cheques are lost or stolen the world's biggest travellers cheque company, American Express, say they can replace them within 24 hours unless you insist on travelling up the Amazon in a canoe. In practice it may be longer, especially if you lose them over the weekend.

Thomas Cook, another big international issuer of travellers cheques, and part of the Midland Bank, have a similar pledge.

If you bank with the Midland you will automatically get Thomas Cook travellers cheques. The other clearing banks issue their own, although often in conjunction with one of the big travellers cheque companies.

Travellers cheques aren't cheap. Your bank or travel company charge a percentage commission when you buy them. And if you cash them at a bank there is a further charge. None the less you usually get a better deal on the exchange rate when you cash travellers cheques at a bank rather than in a shop, hotel or restaurant.

CREDIT CARDS

If you carry a Visa or Access card you can use it to go shopping or draw cash from any shop or bank which displays the Visa symbol, or Mastercard symbol in the case of Access. And if you can remember your PIN number your card works on any cash dispenser designed to take your card. When you draw cash, you are charged the normal amount for a cash withdrawal plus an extra handling charge by the foreign bank.

Before you set out on holiday make sure you know what to do if any of your cheque books, bits of plastic or travellers cheques go astray. You may find you have to telephone three separate numbers if you lose your Eurocheque, travellers cheques and credit card. Most of the numbers will be in the United Kingdom, so make sure you know the international dialling codes from the place you are staying.

# 9

# BUYING A HOME

The psychologists tell us that, next to the death of a close relative, moving house is one of life's most stressful events. And unlike a death in the family, we have no one to blame but ourselves.

What is it that makes us uproot ourselves? Why do we put ourselves through the harrowing ordeal of putting our beloved homes on the market only to have hordes of strangers ridicule our taste?

Why do we spend endless weekends house hunting and trying ever so hard to find something nice to say about houses which we know we hate as soon as we put one foot past the front door?

Why are we willing to abandon all those good neighbours who feed the cat, and babysit the children?

The reason of course is we all need a roof over our heads, and for those of us who can afford it, buying a home of our own is the most practical way of securing this most basic right. But there is no doubt that buying a house and borrowing money to do it, is also about making money. In fact it is the favourite way we British have of acquiring personal wealth.

The number of homes which are owner-occupied rose from 42 per cent in 1961 to 63 per cent in 1987. Getting our foot on that first rung of the home ownership ladder is the most significant financial move of our lives. It can also look like the most difficult, especially when house prices are booming and they keep on moving the goal posts.

According to the Halifax, Britain's largest building society, there are enormous discrepancies between house prices, depending on

# HOME BUYERS

## CHOOSING THE RIGHT MORTGAGE IS AS EASY AS READING THIS AD.

In fact it's even easier, because Keywest Life and Pensions will do it for you.

Being an independent broker means we can choose from the widest range of mortgage options and find you the most competitive rates. So you don't have to wade through miles of information to get the best deal. We can even get you a mortgage at four times your salary. And we're fast too.

If it's just advice you're after, then you can rely on ours as being both comprehensive and totally independent.

So if you're buying a house, or just thinking about it, contact Keywest Life and Pensions. It's the best move you'll make.

**Keywest**
LIFE & PENSIONS

**SOUTH-EAST 01 407 5555**  **NORTH/MID 0274 734124**
**SOUTH-WEST 0272 225641**  **SCOTLAND 031 2200494**

COVERING BRITAIN  (FIMBRA MEMBER)

where you want to live.

For example at the end of 1987 first-time buyers in the North, one of the cheapest places to buy a house, were able to get a 90 per cent mortgage on the average house if they earned £9,150 a year. If they wanted to buy a similar house in Greater London, where houses can be two and a half times more expensive, they needed to be earning £22,875 a year.

That is why in areas where buying your own home is expensive, people club together to buy a flat to share.

## How much can you borrow?

Where do first-time buyers start sorting out the mass of financial detail which they must master before being handed the key to their own front door?

Finding out how much you have to spend is the first step. You are normally able to borrow up to three times your yearly salary. If you are borrowing jointly with someone else the figure will probably be around $2\frac{1}{4}$ per cent of your joint incomes. Or if the figure works out significantly different, three times the larger salary plus a half the lower one.

You can normally borrow up to 90 per cent of the value (not the price) of the house. The figure will be lower if the house needs a lot of work doing to it, although you can increase the mortgage later on.

You will have to find the other 10 per cent out of your savings. But if you fall short don't despair, you may be able to get a top-up mortgage from an insurance company or a bank. Only do this if you are absolutely sure you can afford it.

## How much does it cost to move?

Never underestimate the amount of money it costs to buy a house. Find out just how much by working through this checklist.

- Unless you have plenty of time on your hands and have the energy to learn how to do your own conveyancing, you will have to pay someone to do it for you. Most people use a solicitor, although you can now use a licensed conveyancer. If you know a firm of solicitors ask them for a rough estimate of how much they charge, and how long they take. Compare the cost with that of a licensed conveyancer.
- Ask a surveyor how much it will cost to do a structural survey with a written report on properties in your price range. You don't have to have a structural survey, but it is a wise precaution.

BUYING A HOME

# Over the next 25 years would you prefer to pay a fortune ...

*½% Repayments BELOW Your Best Offer - Guaranteed!

*For first year.

# ... or to save one?

The answer's as obvious as your choice of mortgage consultant ... We guarantee the lowest net repayments in the area. Can forward up to 3 times your joint income. And offer you a 100% mortgage.

Our informative new brochure brings you full details of Rossendale Investments Mortgages. Send for your copy today. And congratulate yourself year after pound-saving year.

## Rossendale
## Investments

50, Bank Street, Rawtenstall, BB4 8DY.
Tel: Rossendale (0706) 211336

*Appointed Financial Adviser of London and Manchester Assurance Co. Ltd.*

I prefer to save a fortune over the next few years. Rush me my free copy of your mortgage guide by return of post.

Name .................................................................

Address .............................................................

........................................................................

Also tell me about (please tick)
Pensions ☐  Personal Finance ☐  Investments ☐

**Mortgage & Finance Brokers • Insurance & Pension Consultants • Personal Financial Planners.**

## ALAN PRESTON & COMPANY
### CAN OFFER YOU A COMPLETE FINANCIAL SERVICE

### MORTGAGES & REMORTGAGES
Raise ONE loan on your home to consolidate all your outstanding debts to reduce your monthly outlay, pay school fees, buy a holiday villa, improve your home.

### MOVING
With us the issue is not clouded by house sales. Let us give you a quote YOU are our concern

### PENSIONS FOR
THE SMALL COMPANY — A NEW approach — No Auditors, Trustees and Costly Admin.
THE EMPLOYER IN A COMPANY SCHEME — We put you in CONTROL. THE SELF EMPLOYED — Don't leave it too late

### INVESTMENTS
Lump Sum Investments Placed for Growth and Income. Income Scheme for Home Owning Pensioners

### PRIVATE HEALTH INSURANCE
It's cheaper than you think —
For an Informal chat without obligation telephone

### COLCHESTER 76004

Appointed Representative of
**Sun Alliance Life**
Applied to LAUTRO & IMRO

3rd Floor, Centurion House
St John's Street
Colchester
Essex CO2 7AN.

A Member of the Paul Hanson Group, Associated Offices in Tamworth, Nuneaton Northampton, Norwich, Gt Yarmouth, Plymouth, Chelmsford and Southend

---

# How Secure is your Financial future ...?

### Plan now for a secure future ...

Badgers Financial Services are specialists in all aspects of personal finance. For a no obligation friendly chat on how we can help call

**Gary Warby 01-547 1010**

We can put it all together

**Badgers**
· FINANCIAL · SERVICES ·

181 Clarence Street
Kingston Upon Thames, Surrey

Appointed Representative of Sun Alliance Life
Applied to LAUTRO and IMRO

Surveyors see things you can't and they know all the tricks people use to cover up defects. And if something does go wrong, and the surveyor should have noticed it, you have someone to sue.
- Ask your lenders how much they charge for doing their survey and for legal fees and whether there are any other fees. You can sometimes save money by getting the lender's surveyor to do the full structural survey for you.
- The cost of moving. First-time buyers can often save here. If you don't have much furniture yet, you can probably get by with a self-drive van and a couple of beefy friends to do the lifting. Otherwise get quotations from several removal firms.
- Stamp duty, if any. There is no stamp duty to pay if the property you buy is worth less than £30,000. If it's worth more you pay 1 per cent. Stamp duty is paid when you buy a house, but not when you sell it.

Once added up, the expense of buying even the smallest flat could come to between £750 and £1,000. It may force you to downgrade your initial estimate of how much money you actually have to spend on buying that home of your dreams.

## Where to go for a mortgage

A mortgage is a loan. The property you buy with it offers the lender security.

Most people get their mortgages from either a bank or a building society. The competition between the banks and the building societies is now so keen that you shouldn't have too much difficulty in getting a mortgage even if you want to buy something unusual. Unless, that is, you choose to buy a house when mortgage funds are in short supply.

It is always worth checking when you start saving with a building society whether there are any kinds of property they won't lend on. A very few building societies don't like flat conversions, while others turn their noses up at houses with a sitting tenant, short leaseholds, timber-framed or thatched houses, or former industrial buildings. Very few lenders consider freehold flats.

It's always worth saving with a couple of building societies, just in case you find yourself buying at a time of mortgage famine. When this happens, building societies tend to give their managers a quota of money to lend each month. If you get to them after they have spent it, you must wait a month before you get an answer, and you may lose your home to another buyer. With several building societies you have more than one iron in the fire.

# MAXIMUM CHOICE MORTGAGES

FROM

**MORTON** **Brian Morton** & Company

**BRIAN MORTON FINANCIAL SERVICES LTD**
32–34 ARTHUR STREET
BELFAST

## TEL: (0232) 244799

Northern Ireland's Largest
The True Professionals · 24 Offices Province Wide

---

## *Sovereign Financial Services*

- Mortgages
- Raising money by Remortgage
- Life Assurance
- Investment ● Pension Schemes
- Commercial Mortgages

For a friendly, personal, professional service telephone

## WARRINGTON (0925) 59048

*Sovereign Financial Services*
41 Winwick Street, Warrington, Cheshire WA2 7TT.

Most of the time you are spoilt for choice, so shop around for the best bargain. Investigate how much your bank or building societies will lend you, and at what rate.

You could even try a bank or building society where you don't have an account, or one of the new entrants into the mortgage market. In the last couple of years a number of insurance companies including some of the largest, such as the Prudential, the Pearl and Commercial Union have started offering mortgages.

And then there are the new mortgage companies – such as the Mortgage Corporation and National Home Loans – which raise their mortgage funds by selling fixed interest mortgage bonds to the public.

When you have decided which offers the best deal for you, ask for a mortgage application form and put in your formal request for a mortgage. Don't make several mortgage applications to different lenders – you only end up paying several lots of surveyor's fees.

## Finding the right mortgage

Choosing the right mortgage to suit you can be a nightmare. There are three main types:

- repayment mortgages
- endowment mortgages
- pension mortgages.

Whatever your mortgage most people get the tax relief on their repayments through the MIRAS system which stands for *Mortgage Interest Relief at Source*. With MIRAS you don't have to claim the tax relief every year from the Inland Revenue. This is done by the lender. An adjustment is made automatically to your mortgage payments.

## Repayment mortgages

You can get a repayment mortgage either from a bank or a building society. With this type of mortgage part of each monthly payment is interest and part is repayment of the loan. In the early years you pay mostly interest. The interest element in each repayment decreases over the course of the mortgage term, until you are repaying mostly capital, and little interest.

You only get tax relief on the interest payments, not on the repayments of capital. It used to be the case that the net repayments after tax increased over the course of the mortgage as the element for interest in each repayment reduced.

## MORTGAGES

100% loans freely available

Interest Rates below Building Society charges

High Income Multiples

Low start payment methods (deferred interest)

Special schemes for professional applicants

**BHW** — **BUDD HULBERT WILLIAMS LTD.**
0734 343900

## CASTLE SPENCER & FISCH
### *SOLICITORS*

Russell House, 19 St. Paul's Street,
Leeds LS1 2JG
Tel: (0532) 434521. Fax: (0532) 453967.

A complete range of services for corporate, institutional and private clients.

*(Written quotations available on request for domestic conveyancing)*

Now most building societies use what is known as the *constant net level repayment* method. Under MIRAS the tax relief can be evened out throughout the mortgage term and the net repayments only alter if there is a change in the mortgage rate. Most building societies use this method for working out the size of your repayments.

Most banks, on the other hand, favour the old method, known as *gross profile*. Bank mortgage repayments usually increase year by year, as the interest element, and thus the tax relief, decreases.

## Endowment mortgages

Endowment mortgages are a method of repaying your mortgage loan with the help of an insurance policy. It is confusing because you still make your mortgage application to a bank or a building society, not directly to an insurance company, unless you have decided to borrow from one.

With an endowment mortgage you borrow the money just as if you were taking out a repayment mortgage. But this time you take out an endowment insurance policy as well. Instead of repaying the loan bit by bit you use the proceeds of the insurance policy to repay the loan at the end of the mortgage term, which is generally after 25 years. If you die before the loan is repaid, the life insurance pays off the loan.

You can normally only take out an endowment mortgage if you have at least 25 years to go before you retire. So they really only work for men under 40 and women under 35.

The only policy worth considering is the type known as the *low cost endowment mortgage*. The repayments aren't much more expensive than with a repayment mortgage, and there are circumstances when they actually work out cheaper, and the value of the policy after 25 years should be larger than the amount needed to repay the loan, giving you a useful lump sum to spend on other things.

## Pension mortgages

Pension mortgages can be a good deal for the self-employed or those who don't have a company pension plan. Instead of using a life insurance policy to repay the mortgage, you use part of the cash sum provided at retirement by a personal pension plan. You get tax relief on your mortgage interest payments in the normal way. But because it's classified as a pension scheme, you also get tax relief on your payments into the pension scheme.

# ALL UNDER ONE ROOF!

At THE SOLICITORS PROPERTY CENTRE, CRAWLEY, we have always offered a complete residential sales and conveyancing service. Now — from our new larger premises, we have opened our Residential Letting and Management Department.

We may have grown a lot over the last 2½ years but our service is as friendly and efficient as ever. Make a Smooth Move and call into our exciting new showroom in the centre of Crawley.

Solicitors participating in the Centre are:
**Burstows**
**Stevens Drake & Pope**
**Glover Bannister & Co.**
**Tarran Jones & Co.**
**Maybury & Sagoo**
**MacArthur & Co.**

**SOLICITORS**
*Property Centre*

**SOLICITORS PROPERTY CENTRE**
49 High Street
Crawley
RH10 1BQ
Telephone 0293 548585
OPEN 7 DAYS A WEEK

---

# CASTLE ASSET MANAGEMENT

■ INVESTMENT MANAGEMENT
■ PENSIONS ■ SCHOOL FEES PLANNING
■ MORTGAGES

Contact: P.A. Bolger. B.A.(Hons.) Econ.
T.D. Allum. B.Sc.(Hons.). Econ.

Telephone: Reigate (0737) 222913
9a West Street, Reigate, Surrey. RH2 9BS
Independant Financial Advisers

So how do you find your way through this mortgage maze? If you are self-employed or don't have a company pension plan, look first at a pension mortgage.

Everyone else must decide whether to go for an endowment mortgage. Building societies and banks earn commission from the insurance company each time they sell an endowment mortgage, so don't let them rush you into a hasty decision.

If you find out the following three things you are well on the way to making an informed decision:

- *The flat rate of interest.* There used to be something called the mortgage rate, when all building societies charged the same amount. Now the banks and building societies compete there is no longer a recommended mortgage rate and there may be slight differences in the rates charged.
- *The APR or true cost of borrowing.* Always ask for this figure. You may find that it gives a different picture from just comparing the flat rates. The true rate of borrowing is the one to trust. The difference arises because the banks and building societies differ in the way they charge interest, and any arrangement fees must be worked into the cost of borrowing.
- *The amount of the monthly repayments.* Check the method used for calculating the repayment. Is it the constant net level or gross profile method? Find out by asking if the repayments stay constant or increase over the period of the loan.

The building societies used to charge a higher rate of interest for endowment mortgages, but competition with the banks slashed that differential. Now the banks and the building societies usually charge the same rate of interest for both repayment and endowment mortgages.

There is not much difference when you compare the monthly repayments. With the mortgage rate at 10 per cent, the Nationwide Anglia Building Society, one of the largest, charges £202.93 a month after tax relief for a loan of £30,000 repaid over 25 years.

Compare this with a 25-year endowment mortgage taken out by someone age 30 with Equitable Life, a company with a good investment record, and you arrive at monthly repayments after tax of £219.25 a month with the insurance policy costing £41.75 and the interest payments £177.50.

The repayment mortgage works out marginally cheaper, but there is no life insurance to pay off the loan if you die early. If you are single with no one dependent on your income, you probably don't mind. Some banks insist that you take out some life insurance. If you

MANAGING YOUR MONEY

# You choose the objective. We'll supply the cover.

Whether you choose between a straight repayment mortgage, an endowment mortgage or a pension mortgage to purchase your new home, General Accident will provide you with the means to secure it.

The choice is yours. Whichever you decide, General Accident has the policy that will best suit you.

**SAVE TODAY - SECURE TOMORROW**

**GA Life**

## General Accident

General Accident Life Assurance Ltd · General Accident Linked Life Assurance Ltd.
2 Rougier Street · YORK YO1 1HR.

lautro

don't want insurance go to a lender who doesn't insist.

But if you have a family you need a mortgage protection policy, which pays off the outstanding loan if you die early. These policies are cheap. Equitable Life charge £3.83 a month for a man age 30. It is slightly cheaper for a woman. This brings the total cost of a repayment mortgage up to £206.76.

Life insurance companies make the figures on endowment mortgages look very attractive. The projection you get shows how much money you can expect to get when the policy matures. The figure shown is usually a lot bigger than the amount needed to repay the mortgage. Don't get too excited, the sum is by no means guaranteed, and in 25 years' time when you finally get your hands on it, inflation will have taken more than a hefty nibble. For example, even if inflation continued to run at only 3 per cent a year for the foreseeable future, £1,000 would be worth less than £500 in 25 years' time.

In the example above, Equitable Life's quotation gives a figure of £38,231 as the value of the policy after 25 years if the level of yearly bonuses increases by 9 per cent a year. This would give you a profit of £8,231 after you repaid the mortgage loan of £30,000. If the bonuses increased by 10¾ per cent a year, the policy would be worth £48,496 after 25 years.

Insurance companies also pay terminal bonuses which are added to the policy only when it is cashed in. Terminal bonuses are the more speculative and unknown element in the calculation. They depend on how profitable the life insurance company has been while the policy is in force. Insurance companies are no longer permitted to give projections which include the value of terminal bonuses and they cannot use a figure of more than 10¾ per cent a year when they project the value of annual bonuses.

But there is no doubt that the promise of some money is better than none. And there is no getting away from the fact that repayment mortgages offer you nothing once the mortgage is paid off.

None the less, while endowment mortgages are now an attractive prospect for a great many home buyers, there are others who should steer well clear. And you won't normally be able to get an endowment mortgage unless there is at least 25 years to go before you retire.

Endowment mortgages have two big disadvantages – they are not very flexible and you won't get all your money back if you surrender the policy in the first 10 years. With endowment mortgages, if there is a big increase in the mortgage rate, you can't bring down the cost

MANAGING YOUR MONEY

# ABINGDON (FIMBRA MEMBER)

INSURANCE, MORTGAGE & PROPERTY SERVICES

## 100% MORTGAGES

- 4 × INCOME
- RE-MORTGAGES FOR ANY PURPOSE
- SELF EMPLOYED/SELF CERT/NON STATUS
  SUBJECT TO STATUS

Outlets through most leading banks and building societies

## FAST, EFFICIENT, INDEPENDENT SERVICE

Also arranged:
All classes of Life Assurance & Pensions

*Just contact Nigel Cottee or Francois Pascal*

269 LONDON ROAD SOUTH, LOWESTOFT, SUFFOLK NR33 0DS
### TEL: LOWESTOFT (0502) 516013

---

## MORTGAGE OR REMORTGAGE

### DOMESTIC AND COMMERCIAL

WE ARE IN CONSTANT TOUCH WITH ALL THE MAJOR
LENDING SOURCES AND CAN OFFER YOU THE MOST
COMPETITIVE RATES AVAILABLE
A FAST EFFICIENT SERVICE WITH THE MAXIMUM ADVANCES
AVAILABLE

### NORTH WALES MORTGAGE & INVESTMENT CENTRE

22, Church Street, Beaumaris, Anglesey, Gwynedd LL58 8AB
(0248) 810491
7, Queens Road, Craig-y-Don, Llandudno, Gwyned LL30 1AZ
(0492) 74831
Glyn Dwr, Castle Street, Ruthin Clwyd LL15 1DP
(08242) 3019
31, Holyhead Road, Upper Bangor, Gwynedd LL57 2EU
(0248) 353567

MORTGAGE BROKERS      (FIMBRA MEMBER)     INVESTMENT CONSULTANTS

of your monthly repayments by arranging to pay off the mortgage over a longer period. You can with a repayment mortgage.

So don't take out an endowment mortgage if:

- you can't afford to increase your mortgage repayments if mortgage rates go up.
- you might want to surrender your policy early. This can happen if you are going to live abroad or you are getting married and your partner already has an endowment mortgage.
- you are self-employed in which case you should be thinking about linking your mortgage to your pension and getting extra tax benefits.

If you decide to go for an endowment policy, you can ask your bank or building society for a quotation. They will provide you with a quotation from a company of their choice. But you are free to do some further shopping around if you want. If you find a life insurance company which offers cheaper premiums you can ask your lender if they would accept the policy. In most cases they will.

You could also ask a mortgage broker to get you several quotations too. Mortgage brokers earn their living from the commission they get from insurance companies when they sell a policy. If you do ask a mortgage broker for quotations, they may try to persuade you to buy a policy from them. Remember you are free to say no. When you ask a mortgage broker for a quotation, you are under no obligation to buy a policy from him.

Mortgage brokers also have their uses if you are finding it difficult to get a mortgage. For example, you may be self-employed, or you may be trying to buy a really way out building, or one with some commercial use, such as a guest house or a pub.

If you are self-employed, the banks and building societies normally ask you to provide the last three years' accounts approved by an accountant. If you can't do this, you may not get your mortgage.

You may want to chuck in your job and start a guest house, for example. Most conventional lenders will turn you down. Mortgage brokers are used to dealing with problems like these. They know the lenders who are prepared to lend to the self-employed, or on oddball and unusual properties.

You may find you pay a higher rate of interest. But it's a price you may not mind paying for actually getting a mortgage. A mortgage broker usually suggests you take out an endowment or pension-linked mortgage. After all they earn their money from the commission they get from the insurance company. However, most mortgage brokers arrange repayment mortgages too, but they ask for a fee for doing it.

# Ralph & Co Solicitors

**FOR ADVICE ON:**

- **DOMESTIC AND COMMERCIAL CONVEYANCING**
- **MORTGAGE ADVICE**
- **FINANCIAL PLANNING**
- **TAXATION**
- **TRUSTS**
- **INHERITANCE TAX**

CALL AT:

18/20 CLIFF ROAD, NEWQUAY TR7 1SG
Telephone: (0637) 872218

52 MOLESWORTH STREET, WADEBRIDGE
Telephone: (020881) 2284

19 ST FRANCES STREET, TRURO TR1 3DW
Telephone: (0872) 72348

32 DUKE STREET, PADSTOW
Telephone: (0841) 532375

## The buying process

When you find the home you want to buy, your first step is making an offer. In England and Wales (the law is different in Scotland) this offer doesn't commit you to buy the house, so long as you make it clear that it is *subject to contract and survey*.

If your offer is accepted, you may be asked for a small returnable deposit which you can agree to lodge with a trustworthy intermediary; the sellers' estate agent or solicitor are the most usual. Remember you are under no legal obligation to hand over any money at this stage, and you should under no circumstances hand over any money directly to a private seller.

The conveyancing of the property can now begin. A conveyance is the legal term used for a contract which is drawn up for the sale and purchase of a property. The solicitors' stranglehold over conveyancing is now broken. You can use a solicitor or a licensed conveyancer to do your conveyancing. You also have the right to do your own conveyancing when you are buying and selling your own home.

Drawing up the draft contract and asking questions about the house make up the first stage of the conveyance. You need to know if anyone has planning permission to build a house overlooking your back garden, or drive a motorway past your front gate. While this is being done, put in your application for a mortgage advance, and if you have decided to carry out a full structural survey, find a surveyor to do it.

EXCHANGING CONTRACTS

Once your mortgage advance is through and you are satisfied that all your questions are answered and your structural survey is satisfactory, you are ready to proceed to the next stage of *exchanging contracts*.

Of course, if your survey finds dry rot or subsidence, you may want to pull out at this stage. But assuming this isn't the case, you are still free to bargain over the price. The survey may show that the house needs some repairs. You can now make the seller a lower offer to take account of this. The seller is equally free to reject it. If you do agree a revised price, you can go ahead and exchange contracts.

Once you have exchanged contracts you are committed to buying the property. You must put down a deposit of 10 per cent of the purchase price which you won't get back if you then fail to buy the property.

You may need to arrange a *bridging loan* with your bank to pay for the deposit. This often happens if you are selling a house as well as buying one. Bridging loans are short-term loans. The interest rate is similar to that charged on arranged overdrafts, ie between 2 and 5

## PROPERTIES·LONDON·LIMITED

### SELL FAST
### OR
### YOUR MONEY BACK!

For just £295+VAT we guarantee to sell your house or flat in less than 4 months or we'll give you £245 back!

C&R Properties Ltd. have developed a unique way to sell cheaply and quickly. There are other options which may be even cheaper!

As a free service, we can find you any type of property from £40,000 to over £100,000 anywhere around London and the Home Counties.

**RING**

## 01-251 6400 for details

C&R PROPERTIES LTD.
287 CITY ROAD
EC1.

per cent above bank base rate.

Even though the house isn't yours yet, the building becomes your responsibility once you have exchanged contracts. So remember to take out buildings insurance to be effective as soon as you exchange contracts. See Chapter 7, *Insurance*.

MORTGAGE GUARANTEE POLICIES
Banks and building societies normally lend up to 90 per cent of their valuation of a property. None the less, lenders never like taking risks, and if they lend you more than 80 per cent, they will ask you to take out something called a mortgage guarantee policy. This covers them against loss on the proportion of your mortgage above 80 per cent of valuation.

If you run into financial difficulties and can't keep up your mortgage payments, your lender may repossess your house. If your lender then sells your house at a loss, he can look to the insurance company to pay the proportion of the loan which is insured.

The cost of a mortgage guarantee policy is usually added to the size of your mortgage advance. The amount is usually small, so most people accept the policy sold them by their lender. You do have the right to ask for alternative quotations.

COMPLETION
Now you are ready to agree a *completion date*. This is the big day: the day you finally buy the house, hand over the rest of the money, and most exciting of all, get the keys to the door.

The gap between exchanging contracts and completion is traditionally 28 days, but it can take any time both parties agree. It can be as quick as the same day, while a delay of a year is by no means unheard of.

# Making a will

Few people ever get round to making a will. Some people think they are immortal, others that it's tempting fate. Don't bury your head in the sand and don't be superstitious. Without a will your money could end up in the wrong hands.

Buying your first home is a good time to think about making a will. You are acquiring a sizable asset, especially if you have life insurance to pay off any outstanding mortgage if you die early.

When you make a will you write down who is to get what, and you hope there won't be any arguments. If you don't make a will you are said to die *in testate*. The rules of intestacy are complicated. As a general rule your belongings are inherited by your next of kin. So if you are single, they go in the first instance to your parents. If your parents are no longer alive, your brothers and sisters and their children are the next to inherit.

Life becomes much more complicated once you get married. It is a common fallacy that a husband's belongings are automatically inherited by his wife, and vice versa.

If there are children they are entitled to inherit a proportion. This can occasionally cause enormous problems, with the family home having to be sold to pay the children. If you make a will you avoid this. The commonest solution is for husbands to leave everything to their wives, and wives to leave everything to their husbands. The children inherit when the last surviving parent dies.

It may not happen very often, but it can happen that a husband and wife die together, say in a car crash. When it isn't clear who died first, the rules of intestacy assume the elder of the two died first. It follows that the younger inherits from the elder, and both estates are inherited by the younger person's next of kin. If you are married without children, there is therefore a remote possibility that your possessions could be passed on to your mother-in-law. This may not be quite what you intend.

---

## B.P.Bonnar A.P.C.S.

### MORTGAGE & FINANCE BROKERS

**100% MORTGAGES**
*(DECISION WITHIN 24 HOURS)*

**MORTGAGES ARRANGED VIA ALL LEADING BUILDING SOCIETIES & BANKS**

* LOW INTEREST RATES FOR HOUSE PURCHASE. LOW START PAYMENT MORTGAGES AVAILABLE

* UP TO 100% OF PURCHASE PRICE (SUBJECT TO STATUS)
* 1ST & 2ND TIME BUYERS
* DOMESTIC & COMMERCIAL
* FINANCE AVAILABLE FOR ALL PURPOSES

Legal & General
Appointed Representative
Legal & General is a member of LAUTRO

**WRITTEN QUOTATIONS FREE**

**051-227 1286**     **051-236 8480**

Suite 419-421, The Corn Exchange, Fenwick Street, L2 7UL

BUYING A HOME

# SPECIAL PROPERTIES DESERVE SPECIAL TREATMENT

## LET OUR COMPUTER SEARCH OUT YOUR BEST MORTGAGE NATIONWIDE

Low start and 100% loans, deferred interest payments, non status mortgages. High earnings multiples. Residential and Commercial Mortgages.

## SPECIAL REDUCED RATES FOR ENDOWMENT AND PENSION MORTGAGES OVER £30,000.

(FIMBRA)

**ASK FOR LES CRAWFORD B.Sc**
**FAIRWOOD INDEPENDENT FINANCIAL ADVISERS**

---

## BUY WISELY

### PROTECT YOUR INVESTMENT WITH RICS HOUSE BUYERS REPORTS

Structural Surveys
Bank Valuations
Insurance Valuations and Claims

Your house is possible the largest investment you will ever make.
Ensure you are buying wisely and safely.
Our Chartered Surveyor Service will provide you with a professional comprehensive and prompt reports on all types of property.
We offer a nationwide service for structural surveys and valuations and RICS Reports throughout South Wales.
ASK FOR IAIN DAY OR CHRIS STEVENS, ARICS, CHARTERED BUILDING SURVEYOR

**FAIRWOOD**  FAIRWOOD HOUSE, 86 EVERSLEY ROAD, SKETTY
SWANSEA, WEST GLAMORGAN SA2 9DF
0792-205640/203211

MANAGING YOUR MONEY

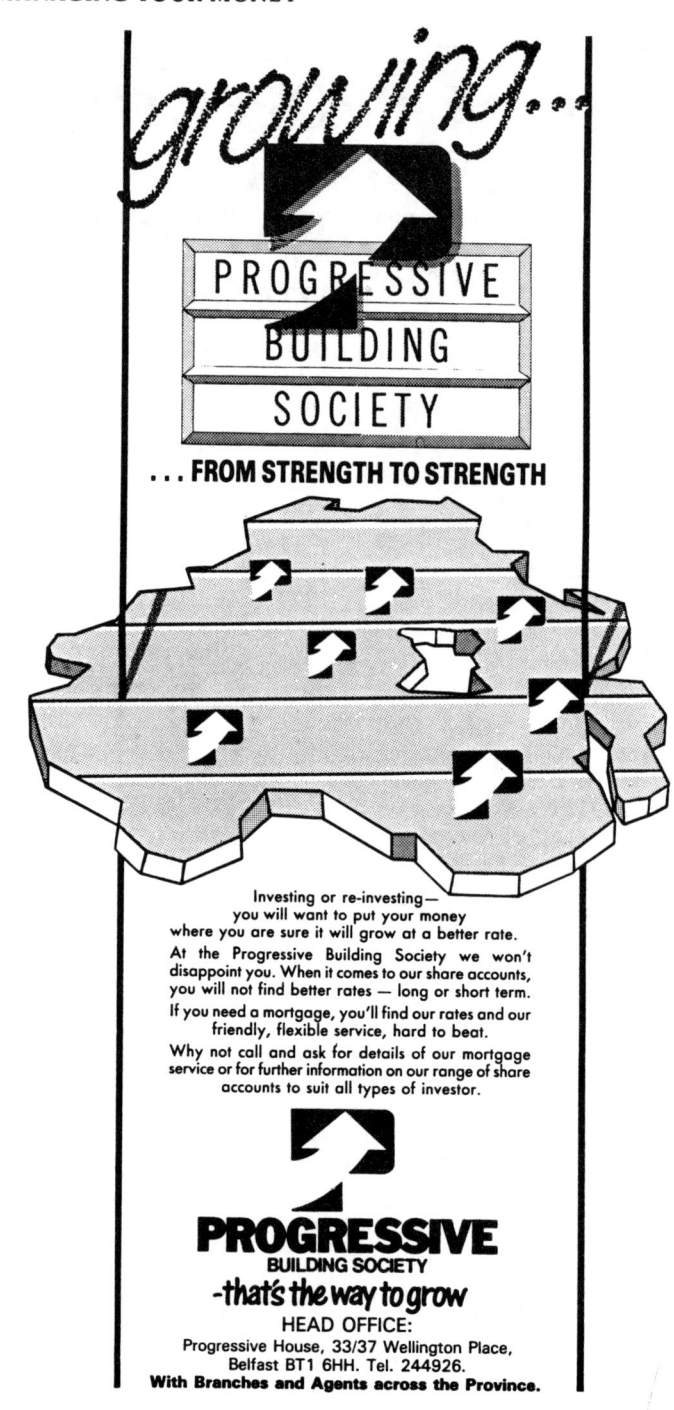

# growing...
## PROGRESSIVE BUILDING SOCIETY
### ...FROM STRENGTH TO STRENGTH

Investing or re-investing—
you will want to put your money
where you are sure it will grow at a better rate.
At the Progressive Building Society we won't disappoint you. When it comes to our share accounts, you will not find better rates — long or short term.
If you need a mortgage, you'll find our rates and our friendly, flexible service, hard to beat.
Why not call and ask for details of our mortgage service or for further information on our range of share accounts to suit all types of investor.

## PROGRESSIVE
**BUILDING SOCIETY**
*-that's the way to grow*

HEAD OFFICE:
Progressive House, 33/37 Wellington Place,
Belfast BT1 6HH. Tel. 244926.
**With Branches and Agents across the Province.**

## BUYING A HOME

### THE FIRST TO SEEK IS ADVICE...

- MOTOR INSURANCE, PRIVATE AND COMMERCIAL 3, 6 & 12 MONTH POLICIES. INSTALMENT PLANS AVAILABLE
- **MORTGAGES 100% ALSO RE-MORTGAGES, DOMESTIC — SEMI COMMERCIAL FOR ANY PURCHASE, CONSOLIDATION OF DEBTS ETC.**
- PENSIONS, PRIVATE, GROUP AND SELF ADMINISTERED
- HOME AND CONTENTS ● SHOPKEEPERS ● CHAUFFEUR PLAN INSURANCE ARRANGED FOR THE CONVICTED DRIVER
- FINANCE ● SECURED AND UNSECURED LOANS
- CAPITAL INVESTMENT PLANS AND ENDOWMENT SCHEMES
- LIFE, FIRE AND ACCIDENT INSURANCE
- ADVICE AND QUOTATIONS. WRITTEN DETAILS ON REQUEST
- ACCIDENT, SICKNESS & REDUNDANCY COVER

### Whickham
#### Insurance Consultants

**HEAD OFFICE:** 23 FELLSIDE ROAD, WHICKHAM, NEWCASTLE UPON TYNE.
**TYNESIDE (091) 488 0000.**

**BRANCHES:** 2 & 2A BARONESS DRIVE, DENTON BURN, NEWCASTLE UPON TYNE
**TUNESIDE (091) 274 6666**
CORNER OF FORE STREET AND THE MEALMARKET, HEXHAM
**HEXHAM: (0434) 608282**

### WE ARE HERE TO HELP YOU!

# 10

# RETIREMENT

In London, the bus conductors call old age pensioners the 'twearlies', which is shorthand for, 'Am I too early to get on the bus with my free bus pass?'

If the thought of joining the twearlies fills you with horror, think again. Anyone who reaches retirement age has a good chance of living to a ripe old age. Women who retire at 60 can expect to live on average for another 21 years. Men who retire at 65 can expect to live on average for another 13 years. So you will still have a lot of living to do.

A high proportion of old people are forced to live in poverty. Make sure your retirement is spent doing all those things you didn't have time to do when you were building your career or bringing up your family.

Spend a little time now finding out what you can expect to get when you retire, and trying to work out whether or not it will be enough. Remember that once you are retired your outgoings may be lower. For example, if you are buying your house on a mortgage, you will have finished paying it off. And you no longer have the cost of travelling to work.

## State pension

To get the flat-rate old age pension you must have paid sufficient National Insurance contributions during your working life. If you aren't entitled to a full pension, you may get a reduced pension instead.

# RETIREMENT

## Pensions...
### Plan to retire NOW!

Many people look forward to retirement - particularly those who have made financial provision to maintain (or improve) their standard of living in these important years.

Obviously the earlier you start planning the more cost effective this will be - but even if you are near retirement there are ways to improve on your income in the most tax efficient and suitable way.

For further information please contact.

## Rixon Matthews Appleyard

MEMBER OF
**BIIBA**
BRITISH INSURANCE & INVESTMENT BROKERS ASSOCIATION

**FIMBRA** MEMBER

Insurance Brokers & Independent Financial Advisers
Rixon Matthews Appleyard (LPI) Ltd
Exchange Court Lowgate Hull Tel 0482 27605

---

There are two rates of old age pension:

- the single person's pension
- the married man's pension.

If a husband and wife both qualify for a pension they get two single persons' pensions. A married man whose wife doesn't qualify for a pensions in her own right gets the married man's pension.

It can happen that you are better off claiming two single persons' pensions, even if one is paid at a reduced rate, and even if the total comes to less than the married couple's pension. This happens because the wife can claim a tax allowance against her pension, but she can't claim it against the married man's pension.

The State flat-rate pension is not generous. Even if you are spending a lot less, it is difficult to make ends meet if this is your only income. In 1986, 1,800,000 pensioners got supplementary pensions because they couldn't manage on the flat-rate pension alone.

## Company pension schemes

If you work for a private company, you are probably a member of a company pension scheme. A few pension schemes are *non-contributory*,

# F. E. WRIGHT
## PENSIONS & FINANCIAL PLANNING

We offer a complete and expert service covering all aspects of Pensions, Property, Investments, Taxation and Legal Advice, based on a full knowledge of your situation.

IT IS —

1. INDEPENDENT — We are registered independent intermediaries acting as agents on *your* behalf.
2. OBJECTIVE — your objectives, not ours.
3. CLEAR — no jargon

**Please telephone or write to:**

Owen Sweetman, Managing Director
F E Wright Pensions & Financial Planning Ltd
The Lonrho Financial Services Subsidiary
109 Borough High Street
London SE1 1NL
Tel: 01-407 4477

(FIMBRA MEMBER)

for an initial interview without obligation

*FIMBRA — Financial Intermediaries, Managers, Brokers, Regulatory Authority.*
*Society of Pension Consultants, British Insurance & Investment Brokers Association*

---

## A NATIONWIDE SERVICE

# Day–Sudbury
## Associates Ltd.

27 Old Market,
Wisbech, Cambs. PE13 1NB

Telephone: Wisbech (0945) 63701

**FOR ALL YOUR PENSIONS AND LIFE ASSURANCE REQUIREMENTS**

# RETIREMENT

and the scheme is paid for entirely by the company. These days most company pension schemes are *contributory* with both employees and employers paying into the scheme.

If it's a good scheme it will be *contracted out* and you won't have to pay into the State Earnings-Related Pension Scheme (SERPS) as well. If the benefits are restricted it will be *contracted in*, and you will have to be a member of SERPS.

When you join a company pension scheme you will be given a booklet which explains the scheme. Don't stuff it in the back of your desk drawer to gather dust. Keep it safe, read it and make sure you understand it.

Company pension schemes are a good deal for those rare employees who stay with one company from the day they leave school to their retirement at the age of 60 or 65. There is a pension of up to two-thirds the salary in your last years at work, and if you are a married man a reduced pension for your wife when you die. If you are a married woman there can be a reduced pension for a dependant or your husband when you die.

All the best company pension schemes are of the type known as *final salary schemes*. If your pension scheme is like this, your pension will be worked out as a multiple of your salary at or near retirement times the number of years you have been a member of the scheme. Under Inland Revenue rules you can't draw a pension of more than two-thirds your salary at retirement.

The most commonly used multiples are a sixtieth or an eightieth for each year in the pension scheme. So after 40 years in a scheme based on sixtieths, you get a pension of two-thirds your final salary, and half your final salary if you are in a scheme based on eightieths.

When you retire you have the right to take part of your pension as a tax-free lump sum. This reduces your pension, but is usually a good way of saving tax, and most people are advised to take the cash sum.

Job changers don't do so well from company pension schemes. When you change jobs it is difficult deciding what to do with your pension.

There are four options:

- Leave your pension with your old employer and collect it when you retire. You get a pension based on your salary when you leave the job. So if you spent 10 years in a pension scheme based on sixtieths, your pension at retirement is worth one-sixth of your salary when you left the scheme.

  Contracted out pension funds are required to increase the value of any pension you leave behind. This is to make sure that your pension is no less than if you had been in the State Earnings-

MANAGING YOUR MONEY

## RETIRED?

### WE CAN INCREASE YOUR INCOME AND YET PROVIDE GOOD CAPITAL GROWTH!

WE SPECIALISE IN PROVIDING INVESTORS WITH A PERSONAL PORTFOLIO DESIGNED TO MAXIMISE THEIR INCOME ENSURING THAT THEIR CAPITAL MAINTAINS ITS TRUE VALUE AGAINST INFLATION.

**NORTH WALES MORTGAGE & INVESTMENT CENTRE**

22, Church Street, Beaumaris, Anglesey, Gwynedd LL58 8AB
(0248) 810416
7, Queens Road, Craig-y-Don, Llandudno, Gwynedd LL30 1AZ
(0492) 74831
Glyn Dwr, Castle Street, Ruthin, Clwyd LL15 1DP
(08242) 3019
31, Holyhead Road, Upper Bangor, Gwynedd LL57 2EU
(0248) 353567

MORTGAGE BROKERS         FIMBRA MEMBER         INVESTMENT CONSULTANTS

---

### Are you getting the best pensions deal?

Consult Geoff Bailey or Nick Watson at

## Huntrods, Haydon & Rose (Financial Services) Ltd

Armoury House, 45a Otley Street,
Skipton, North Yorkshire BD23 1EL
Tel. 0756 60915

FIMBRA MEMBER

**FOR SPECIALIST ADVICE ON:—**
- COMPANY & PERSONAL PENSIONS
- INVESTMENT COUNSELLING
- RETIREMENT PLANNING

BIIBA MEMBER — BRITISH INSURANCE & INVESTMENT BROKERS' ASSOCIATION

Related Pension Scheme. But there is no guarantee to link it with inflation.

If you decide to leave your pension with your old employer you have the right to change your mind later. You can now request a transfer value at any time up to a year before you retire.

- Transfer it. This is a bit like a football transfer fee, but between pension schemes and with no one wanting to give away more than they have to. If you feel really confident that your new employer is just itching to get you, make the transfer of your pension part of the negotiation.

But if you are a small cog in a large wheel the amount your old pension scheme agrees to transfer into your new pension scheme may not be very generous.

Legally, your old pension fund is obliged to give you a transfer, but your new scheme is under no obligation to accept it, although they invariably will.

- A buy-out bond. This is a relatively new option. Instead of transferring your pension to your new employer's scheme, you can use the money to buy your own scheme (buy-out bond) from an insurance company. This may be a sensible option if the normal run of pension fund doesn't match your circumstances. Single people, for example, don't need widow's or dependant's pensions, so may do better with a buy-out bond.

- A refund of contributions. If you have been paying into your pension fund for less than five years you can take a refund of your own contributions. You don't get the benefit of the money your employer paid into the scheme on your behalf. There is also a deduction of 20 per cent for tax. And if you aren't in SERPS there is a further deduction to buy you back into it.

## Public sector schemes

You are a lucky person if you belong to a public sector scheme. Civil servants and people in the armed services are the main groups to benefit from these schemes which are effectively guaranteed by the government. They pay pensions which rise in line with inflation, the kind of open-ended guarantee which would bankrupt any company scheme.

## The State Earnings-Related Pension Scheme

You pay into the State Earnings-Related Pension Scheme (SERPS) if you aren't a member of a contracted-out company or personal

## BEECH HILL PENSIONS TRUSTEES LIMITED

- Pension Schemes
- Pension Administrators
- Retirement Counselling
- Life & Health Insurance
- Capital Investment
- Mortgage Finance

Let Us Help You With Your Requirements

Contact:
**BEECH HILL PENSION TRUSTEES LIMITED**

2, VICTORIA STREET,
ALTRINCHAM
CHESHIRE WA14 1ET.

Tel 061-928 3820   Telex 665205   Telefax 061-928 3805

Part of the Jefferson Smurfit Group Plc.

Interim Authorised    Applied to F.I.M.B.R.A.

## CASTLE DYKE FINANCIAL SERVICES

CASTLE DYKE HOUSE · 51 HIGHWEEK VILLAGE
NEWTON ABBOT · DEVON TQ12 1QG · Tel: (0626) 52913

REGULATED FOR INVESTMENTS BY THE SECURITIES AND INVESTMENT BOARD

As Independent Financial Advisors we are able to offer FREE impartial advice on all aspects of managing your money

- From individual Pension Schemes to large Group Schemes
- From High Equity non status Mortgages to re-Mortgage facilities for any purpose - all at competitive rates.
- From High Income Multiple and 100% Mortgages to Low Start Schemes with Interest Payment Holidays.
- From a range of excellent performing Broker Managed Funds to Unit Trusts.
- Life Assurance and Inheritance Tax Planning Schemes to suit all needs

pension scheme. Anyone whose employer doesn't provide a pension scheme or whose pension scheme falls below a certain standard is swept into this scheme. Contributions are based on a percentage of salary. To work out your pension, your earnings in each year of your working life are revalued to take account of inflation. You can then calculate an average year's pay. Your State Earnings-Related Pension is a fifth of this figure and falls well below that which could be expected from a good company scheme.

## State graduated scheme

The state graduated scheme preceded the State Earnings-Related Pension Scheme. If you worked between 1961 and 1975 you probably paid into this scheme and are entitled to an extra pension. It may only come to a few pence a week.

## Personal pensions

From the beginning of July 1988 everyone has the right to provide for their own pension through a personal pension. This kind of pension arrangement used to be available only to the self-employed or those working in companies where there was no company pension scheme. Now no employer has the right to make it a condition of your employment that you join the company pension scheme.

Personal pensions offer tax benefits which no other savings plan can beat. You can invest up to 17½ per cent of what you earn tax free. The percentage rises to a maximum of 26½ per cent the older you get. The money grows in a fund which is almost entirely free of tax, and in theory should give a better return than other investments which are taxed.

The disadvantage is that you can only draw a pension when you retire, although there are now widespread provisions for borrowing against the value of the fund if you need to expand your business, or want to buy into a partnership.

You can also tailor the pension scheme to meet your own needs. For example you might want to provide a pension for a dependant.

Personal pensions like the earlier self-employed pensions are a very good deal for the self-employed. However, anyone in a company pension scheme should think long and hard before quitting a company scheme in favour of a personal pension.

The main disadvantage of leaving an employer's scheme is that you are likely to lose the benefit of your employer's contribution.

MANAGING YOUR MONEY

---

## INVESTMENTS

### Wadsworth Bates

**The Independent investment and pensions firm for the future now!**

**IF YOU WANT TO GET IT RIGHT**

for any of the following
contact us at the numbers below

- UNIT TRUSTS
- PENSIONS
- SCHOOL FEES
- PERSONAL EQUITY PLANS
- EXPATRIATE ADVICE
- MORTGAGES

FIMBRA MEMBER

7 CROSSLEY STREET, WETHERBY LS22 4RT. (0937) 62818

29 CARR MANOR GROVE, LEEDS LS17 5YZ (0532) 664992

---

## HANDSCOMBE FINANCIAL & INVESTMENT SERVICES

*For independent professional advice on:*

BIIBA

FIMBRA

Pension Schemes
Unit Trusts
Inheritance Tax Planning
Commercial Loans
School Fees Planning

Mortgages
Life Assurance
Savings Plans
Health Insurance
Capital Investments

*Do contact the experts:*

**Brian E. Handscombe (Life & Pension Brokers) Ltd.
Barratt House, 668 Hitchin Road, Luton, Beds LU2 7XJ
Telephone: Luton (0582) 400202**

Most employers with existing company pension schemes say they won't pay money into employees' personal pension schemes if they decide to quit the company scheme.

Personal pensions are undoubtedly a good idea for the young and footloose. If you think you are going to spend the beginning of your working life changing jobs every couple of years you are likely to do better with a personal pension. After all there is nothing to prevent your joining a company pension scheme once you feel you are settled.

Men above 45 and women over 40 who are already paying into a company pension scheme could damage their pension prospects by opting for a personal pension. If they are worried about the size of their eventual pension, they are probably better off making additional voluntary contributions instead.

## Additional voluntary contributions

You can claim tax relief on money you put towards a company pension, up to a maximum of 15 per cent of your earnings. Most company pension schemes require you to contribute much less than this, usually between 4 and 6 per cent of pay. Additional voluntary contributions (AVCs for short) are a useful way of boosting your company pension. For example, if you contribute 5 per cent to your company pension scheme, you could increase the amount you are providing for your pension by paying AVCs up to a maximum of 10 per cent of earnings.

AVCs are the best way of increasing your pension in the last years of your working life. They are even a good deal if you are younger and your pension looks inadequate and you are fairly sure you will spend the rest of your working life with your present employer.

But don't overdo the AVCs. However much you pay into your scheme remember you can't take a pension of more than two-thirds of your final pay.

You now have the right to set up your own AVC scheme. Instead of paying AVCs to your employer you can now shop around for what has become known as a 'freestanding' AVC scheme which you can buy from an insurance company.

MANAGING YOUR MONEY

# RIGHT FROM THE START!

### THAT'S OUR MOTTO

PLANNING YOUR PENSION IS OF VITAL IMPORTANCE

FOR FRIENDLY, PERSONAL AND PROFESSIONAL ADVICE CONTACT US WITHOUT DELAY — NO OBLIGATION

## R·A·M FINANCIAL SERVICES LTD.

Independent Financial Advisers
Insurance Brokers

20 London Road · Horsham · RH12 1YY
Tel: (0403) 64200

FIMBRA MEMBER

---

For truly independent advice from experienced professionals – our specialists use the most up-to-date computer analysis and market research to provide our clients with effective solutions and best financial advice.

Charles **REYNOLDS & Associates** Ltd

· LIFE ASSURANCE · PENSIONS ·
· MORTGAGES · INVESTMENTS ·
· TAX PLANNING · SAVINGS ·

FIMBRA MEMBER

Associates House, 118 East Barnet Road,
New Barnet, Hertfordshire, EN4 8RE.
Telephone 01-441 6777

RETIREMENT

## *B. J. K. Financial Services*

### IF ALL PENSIONS WERE THE SAME WHY WOULD WE EXIST?

Pension payouts can vary by tens of thousands of pounds, so buying the wrong one can ruin your retirement. As Independent Financial Advisers, we know the market and can make sure you get a good deal. That's why we're here.

66 Boutport Street
Barnstable
North Devon
EX31 1HG
Tel: Barnstable (0271) 46711

FIMBRA MEMBER

---

## *THE "NEW STYLE" CONSULTANTS*
*PERSONAL AND COMPANY ADVICE AVAILABLE*

| INSURANCE | BUSINESS CONSULTANTS | ACCOUNTANCY SERVICES | INVESTMENTS |
|---|---|---|---|
| ↓ | ↓ | ↓ | ↓ |
| PERSONAL CORPORATE PENSIONS | FUNDRAISING (100 LENDERS) | BOOK-KEEPERS | DESIGNED FOR EACH CLIENT |
| ↓ | ↓ | ↓ | ↓ |
| GENERAL AND LIFE | PERSONAL CONTACTS | TAXATION SPECIALISTS | SUBSTANTIAL FUNDS UNDER MANAGEMENT |
| ↓ | ↓ | ↓ | ↓ |

### HAYWARD FINANCIAL SERVICES Limited

214 Desborough Avenue
High Wycombe
Bucks HP11 2TN
Tel: (0494) 463131
Prestel: 844216893
Fax: (0494) 24661

FIMBRA MEMBER

55 North Street
Thame
Oxon OX9 3BH
Tel: (084421) 6891/2/3/4
Prestel: 844216893
Fax: (084421) 5027

# Appendices

# APPENDIX 1

# USEFUL ADDRESSES

*Association of British Insurers (ABI)*
Aldermary House
Queen Street
London EC4N 1TT
Tel: 01-248 4477

*Association of Futures Brokers and Dealers (AFBD)*
B Section, 5 Floor
Plantation House
Mincing Lane
London EC3M 3DX
Tel: 01-626 9763

*Banking Information Service*
10 Lombard Street
London EC3V 9EL
Tel: 01-626 8486

Office of the *Banking Ombudsman*
Citadel House
5-11 Fetter Lane
London EC4A 1BR
Tel: 01-583 1395

*Building Societies Association*
3 Savile Row
London W1X 1AF
Tel: 01-437 0655

*Building Societies Ombudsman*
Grosvenor Gardens House

35-37 Grosvenor Gardens
London SW1X 7AW
Tel: 01-931 0044

*Company Pensions Information Centre*
7 Old Park Lane
London W1Y 3LJ
Tel: 01-493 4757

*Council for Licensed Conveyancers*
Golden Cross House
Duncannon Street
London WC2N 4JF
Tel: 01-210 4604

*Financial Intermediaries, Managers and Brokers Regulatory Association (FIMBRA)*
22-23 Great Tower Street
London EC3R 5AQ
Tel: 01-929 2711

*Inland Revenue*
Somerset House
The Strand
London WC2R 1LB
Tel: 01-438 6622

*Insurance Ombudsman Bureau*
31 Southampton Row
London WC1B 5HT
Tel: 01-242 8613

*The International Stock Exchange*
Old Broad Street
London EC2N 1HP
Tel: 01-588 2355

*Investment Management Regulatory Organisation (IMRO)*
Centre Point
103 Oxford Street
London WC1A 1PT
Tel: 01-379 0601

*Law Society*
113 Chancery Lane
London WC2A 1PL
Tel: 01-242 1222

*Life Assurance and Unit Trust Regulatory Organisation (LAUTRO)*
Centre Point
103 Oxford Street
London WC1A 1PT
Tel: 01-379 0044

*Money Management*
Greystoke Place
London EC4A 1ND
Tel: 01-405 6969

*National Savings*
General Enquiries
Tel: 01-605 9477

*National Savings Bank*
Boydstone Road
Cowglen
Glasgow G58 1SB
Tel: 041-649 4555

*National Savings Certificates and SAYE Office*
Milburngate House
Durham DH99 1NS
Tel: 091-386 4900

*National Savings Stock Register*
Bond and Stock Office
Preston New Road
Marton
Blackpool FY3 9YP
Tel: 0253 66151

*Planned Savings*
150 Caledonian Road
London N1 9RD
Tel: 01-279 6854

*The Securities Association (TSA)*
Old Broad Street
London EC2N 1HP
Tel: 01-588 2355

*Securities and Investments Board (SIB)*
3 Royal Exchange Buildings
London EC3V 3NL
Tel: 01-283 2474

## MANAGING YOUR MONEY

*Tax Payers' Society*
Room 22
1st Floor
Wheatsheaf House
4 Carmelite Street
London EC4Y 0BN
Tel: 01-583 6020

*Unit Trust Association*
65 Kingsway
London WC2B 6TD
Tel: 01-831 0898

# APPENDIX 2

# USEFUL LEAFLETS

## Department of Health and Social Security

| | |
|---|---|
| **CH.1** | Child benefit |
| **FB.9** | Unemployed? |
| **NI.1** | Married women: your National Insurance position |
| **NI.12** | Unemployment benefit |
| **NI.16** | Sickness benefit |
| **NI.16A** | Invalidity benefit |
| **NP.27** | Looking after someone at home: how to protect your pension |
| **NI.27A** | NI contributions: People with small earnings from self-employment |
| **NP.28** | NI contributions |
| **NP.32** | Your retirement pension |
| **NP.32A** | Your retirement pension if you are widowed or divorced |
| **NP.32B** | Retirement benefits for married women |
| **NP.35** | Your benefit as a widow for the first 26 weeks |
| **NP.36** | Your benefit as a widow after the first 26 weeks |
| **NI.40** | NI guide for employees |
| **NI.41** | NI guide for the self-employed |
| **NI.42** | NI voluntary contributions |
| **NI.51** | Widows: guidance about NI contributions and benefits |
| **NI.92** | Earning extra pension by cancelling your retirement |
| **NI.95** | Divorced women: NI guide |
| **NI.196** | Social security benefit rates and earnings rules |
| **NI.208** | National Insurance contribution rates, sick pay and maternity rates |
| **NI.230** | Unemployment benefit and your occupational pension |
| **NI.231** | Made redundant? |
| **NI.244** | Statutory sick pay |
| **NI.246** | How to appeal |

## Inland Revenue

| | |
|---|---|
| **IR4** | Income tax and pensioners |
| **IR4A** | Income tax – age allowance |
| **IR13** | Income tax – wife's earnings election |
| **IR22** | Income tax – personal allowances |
| **IR23** | Income tax and widows |
| **IR24** | Class 4 National Insurance |
| **IR29** | Income tax and one-parent families |
| **IR30** | Income tax – separation and divorce |
| **IR31** | Income tax and married couples |
| **IR32** | Income tax – separate assessment |
| **IR34** | Income Tax – Pay As You Earn |
| **IR41** | Income tax and the unemployed |
| **IR52** | Your tax office – why it is where it is |
| **IR55** | Bank interest – paying tax |
| **IR56** | Tax – employed or self-employed? |
| **IR57** | Thinking of working for yourself? |
| **IR63** | MIRAS Mortgage Interest Relief at Source |

# PERSONAL FINANCE TITLES FROM KOGAN PAGE

*Blackstone Franks Good Investment Guide, The*, David Franks, 1987
*Blackstone Franks Guide to Living in Spain*, 1988
*Blackstone Franks Guide to Perks from Shares*, 1988
*Buying and Selling a House or Flat*, Howard and Jackie Green, 1988
*Cashwise: How to Achieve More from a Fixed Income*, Frank Birkin, 1987
*Easing into Retirement*, Keith Hughes, 1987
*Living and Retiring Abroad*, 2nd edn, Michael Furnell, 1988
*Personal Pensions: The Choice is Yours*, Norman Toulson, 1987

# INDEX OF ADVERTISERS

Abingdon 138
Alan Preston & Co 128
Allied Anglo Financial Services *back cover*
Arthur Marsh & Son (Insurance Brokers) Ltd 100
Ashton Associates 58
Ashton Associates (Kent) 68
Aylesbury Associates 14

Badgers Financial Services 128
Bank of Ireland 57
Beech Hill Pensions Trustees Ltd 154
BJK Financial Services 159
BP Bonnar 144
Brass Castle Consultants Ltd 73
Brian Foster & Associates 59
Brian Morton & Co 130
Budd Hulbert Williams Ltd 132

C & R Properties Ltd 142
Castle Asset Management 134
Castle Dyke Financial Services 154
Castle, Spencer & Fisch 132
Charles Reynolds & Associates 158
Childs & Co 72
Chris Leach & Associates Ltd 64
City Finance 76
Connaught Fine Ltd 68

Day-Sudbury Associates Ltd 150
Deacon Hoare 58
Donne Mileham & Haddock 81

Fairwood Independent Financial Advisers 145
Fleming Associates 62

General Accident Life & Assurance Ltd 136
Godwins Ltd 114

Hamilton Financial Group Ltd, 86, 98
A Hampton & Co 110
Handscombe Financial & Investment Services 156
Hannam Hatton Associates 64
Harald Osthoff & Associates Co Ltd 74
Harold Sharp, Son & Gresty 19
Hayward Financial Services Ltd 159
HSD Business & Family Services 95
Huntrods, Haydon & Rose (Financial Services) Ltd 152
Hurst & Co 19

Independent Financial Services 78

# INDEX

Industrial Funding Trust Ltd 59
Insurance & Mortgage Services Ltd 109
Insurance Service plc, The 102

James Fernley & Partners 112

Ken Ward & Co 84
Keywest Insurance 125

Lacome & Co 27
D Lawson & Son (Insurances) Ltd 106
Leven Financial Services 84

Managed Financial Services Ltd 8
McCaffrey & Co 25
McQuitty/Ross 105
Midas Financial Services 78
Mondial Assistance *inside front cover*
Money Concepts 70
Moore Bedworth & Co 27

North Wales Mortgage & Investment Centre 138, 152

DF Pantry 96
Pendragon Financial Services 20
Phillips Partnership, The *inside back cover*
Pilling & Co 111
Pinhey Barnes & Co 95
Platt (Life & Pensions) Ltd 108
Prestbury Securities 88

Progressive Building Society 146

Ralph & Co 140
RAM Financial Services Ltd 158
Rixon Matthews Appleyard 149
Rossendale Investments 127
RS & J Insurance Services (Wales) Ltd 77

Shaw Heath Insurance Brokers 106
Solicitors Property Centre 134
Sovereign Financial Services 130
Stone Motor Policies 117

Thesis 81
Trumark Financial Services Ltd 78

Union Allied (Insurance Services) 110

Wadsworth Bates 156
PJ Waller 113
Wantage Insurance 100
Whickham 147
Williams & Sherlock 113
Williamson Moore (Investments) Ltd 111
RH Willis & Son 83
Wilmot Dollar Associates 62
HR Wilson & Partners Ltd 109
FE Wright 150

Yorkshire Unit Trust Managers Ltd, The 74